SUNDAY BRUNCH

SUNDAY BRUNCH

Simple, Delicious Recipes for Leisurely Mornings

by **BETTY ROSBOTTOM** | *photographs by* **SUSIE CUSHNER**

CHRONICLE BOOKS

SAN FRANCISCO

Text copyright © 2012 by Betty Rosbottom.
Photographs copyright © 2012 by Susie Cushner.

Library of Congress Cataloging-in-Publication Data available.
ISBN 978-1-4521-0535-2

Manufactured in China

Design & Illustrations by Hillary Caudle
Prop styling by Molly Fitzsimons
Food styling by Carrie Purcell

10 9 8 7 6 5 4 3 2 1

Chronicle Books LLC
680 Second Street
San Francisco, California 94107
www.chroniclebooks.com

DEDICATION

For my grandchildren, Edie and Griffin, who have helped prepare and serve many a pancake, the only dish they think necessary for brunch. With syrup.

ACKNOWLEDGMENTS

Once again I tip my hat to my editor, Bill LeBlond. Thank you for proposing a book on Sunday brunches and for giving me, as always, such valuable and wise counsel.

Thanks to my agent, Lisa Ekus, and her team, most especially Jaimee Constantine, for your unfailing support.

I could not have undertaken this project without the help of my talented assistants, Mary Francis, Emily Bell, Diana Tindall, and Ron Parent. Thank you, Mary, for organizing the testers for this book and for using your brilliant computer skills to make my work so much easier. Many, many hugs to Emily, Diana, Ron, and Mary, too, for the long hours you spent in my kitchen creating and testing dishes.

My thanks to Hanna St. Marie and Claudia Easton, two Amherst College students whose love of food brought them to my kitchen to help test brunch dishes.

Gifted cooks Sheri Lisak and June McCarthy took time to fine-tune my recipes, while talented writer, Ellen Ellis, pored over the text to make my words shine.

A group of volunteers, near and far, tested recipes for this collection, and then wrote detailed reviews. There are not enough words of gratitude for Marilyn Cozad, Lauren Daniels, Kent Faerber, Julia Hanley, Cindy Kurban, Jackie Murrill, Wendy Kersker Ninke, and Betty Orsega. Many thanks also to Marilyn Dougherty, Cindy Pizzanelli, Penny Schacht, and Carroll Vuncannon for your help.

I have been incredibly lucky to work with the creative people at Chronicle Books, who magically transform my electronic manuscripts into beautifully designed cookbooks. Thanks especially to Sarah Billingsley, Doug Ogan, Claire Fletcher, Sara Schneider, Tera Killip, Peter Perez, and David Hawk.

To my family, Mike, Heidi, and those pancake-makers par excellence, Edie and Griffin, thanks for your love.

Last, but never least, thanks to my husband, Ron—a great eater, critic, and editor. You sampled morning food for supper for weeks on end, gave me candid and valuable opinions of recipes, and never—well, almost never—complained when you were asked to edit yet another page of text. You are the best!

TABLE *of* CONTENTS

Introduction

"Brunch is cheerful, sociable and inciting. It is talk-compelling. It puts you in a good temper, it makes you satisfied with yourself and your fellow beings, it sweeps away the worries and cobwebs of the week."

—GUY BERINGER, *Hunter's Weekly* (1895)

I grew up in the South, where an opportunity to entertain is never missed, even early in the day. When I was a young girl in my teens, frequent brunches were a popular way for my friends to get together. Our mothers (bless them!) spent hours preparing these morning fetes, usually held on weekends or during the holidays. The menus would include a mouthwatering array of homemade fare. There were baskets of pastries, scrambled eggs piled high on big platters, baked hams glistening with brilliant glazes, tender biscuits, bowls of fresh fruit salad, and pots of steaming hot coffee. Arranged and served buffet-style, these meals could have fed a multitude. Our parents loved brunches as much as we youngsters did. On fall weekends, they planned late-morning, pregame menus anchored by Southern favorites such as shrimp and grits or luscious stratas. For their own parties, stiffer libations like Bloody Marys were set out alongside the coffee urn.

After college, and newly married, I finally tried my own hand at brunch. My husband and most of our friends were graduate students on limited budgets. It didn't take us long to discover that weekend brunch was an inexpensive yet special way to socialize. I still recall the first invitation we received for Sunday brunch; no meal could have been simpler or more pleasurable. The hosts set the table with crisp linens and good china, but kept the food easy and uncomplicated. That menu is still clearly etched in my memory: there were popovers with butter and homemade jam, freshly squeezed orange juice, creamy scrambled eggs, and sautéed sausages and bacon. We ate, talked, laughed, and lingered at the table for several hours.

My husband and I still plan plenty of morning gatherings, sometimes large-scale ones for bustling crowds, especially around the holidays, but more frequently small, cozy get-togethers with a handful of close friends. Whatever the format, I delight in entertaining at brunch, where the possibilities for creative food and leisurely conversation are endless.

Brunch is, in fact, a relatively new phenomenon. The word itself was coined in 1895 by Guy Beringer. In an article in a British magazine, *Hunter's Weekly*, Beringer proposed a new meal, a blending of both breakfast and luncheon fare to be served around noon on Sunday, often after a morning of hunting. A few years later, brunches began to take hold in the States, and today their popularity spans the globe.

It's easy to understand why. Anything goes when it comes to brunch. You can polish the silver and iron those damask napkins when you want to be fancy, or use your everyday dishes and set the table in the kitchen to keep things light and casual. Start as early or as late in the morning as you like, and encourage guests to stay as long as they want. Menus can be flexible, too. Serve only three or four items, or set out a copious buffet.

The recipes in this collection include classic favorites as well as original creations, but all are versatile enough to fit into whatever brunch menu you're planning. In the chapter devoted to egg cookery, you'll find inspiration for poaching, frying, baking, and scrambling. Another section stars practical, all-in-one baked dishes such as savory tarts with colorful fillings, rich creamy flans, and egg gratins. If you love griddled fare, you'll be tempted to try some sublime pancakes, golden waffles with irresistible toppings, and both baked and pan-sautéed versions of French toast. Fresh seasonal fruits, innovatively prepared, and baked goods, warm from the oven, add special touches to any brunch; you'll find plenty of tempting choices for both. To round out a menu, interesting sides, including smoked fish, hashes, grits, and several potato variations, are ready to complement brunch main courses. A final chapter is dedicated to a variety of drinks. Some are enlivened with spirits, while others are virgin; a few are offered warm, others chilled; and several are perfect for launching a meal, while a couple make fine finales.

While creating and fine-tuning the recipes for this book, I along with a talented coterie of assistants sat down to sample our handiwork at all hours of the day. Sometimes we were biting into warm caramelized shallot and ham tarts at 10 A.M., eating fried eggs on a bed of wild mushrooms at noon, or downing another version of Bloody Marys at three in the afternoon. What we discovered is that brunch fare is gloriously simple and universally appealing. The possibilities for creating interesting recipes to serve at morning meals are endless, but we chose our favorite and best for this collection. I hope the special dishes on the following pages will keep you busy planning Sunday brunches all year long.

COOKING TIPS AND GUIDELINES

EGGS—PERFECT EVERY TIME

Poaching

The easiest way to poach eggs is in an egg poacher pan. This consists of a shallow saucepan with a poaching frame that has cups for the eggs and a lid. The advantage of this neat and efficient method is that it produces softly cooked eggs that are uniform in shape.

Another technique is to cook the eggs in a large, heavy frying pan of simmering water to which 1 tbsp of white vinegar has been added for every 1-qt/960-ml of water. (The vinegar helps the eggs hold together.) The eggs should be added to the pan, one at a time, by breaking each onto a saucer, and then sliding it in. It is also helpful, but not essential, to stir the water with a wooden spoon while the eggs are poaching to help them cook evenly. Cooked eggs are best removed with a slotted spoon or spatula.

Frying

For this quick method, a heavy or nonstick frying pan is a must. You melt butter (count on 1½ to 2 tsp per egg) in the pan over medium heat and, when it is just starting to foam, add the eggs, one at a time, by breaking each onto a saucer, and then sliding it in. The heat should be reduced to low once all the eggs are added. The eggs need to be basted with the warm butter until the whites are set but the yolks still soft.

Scrambling

The secret to extra creamy, moist scrambled eggs is to incorporate bits of butter or cream cheese into the beaten eggs before cooking. Butter or even oil is then heated in a nonstick frying pan set over medium heat. Once the beaten eggs are poured into the pan, they should be stirred constantly, until set but still glistening.

Baking

All you need to make baked or shirred eggs are small individual baking dishes. Crème brûlée dishes or custard cups both work well. You simply butter them, slide in the eggs, and add seasonings. The trick is to check on the eggs once they start to set and take them out when the whites are firm and the yolks are still soft.

Omelet Making

Many people are intimidated by the thought of making omelets, but nothing could be simpler or quicker if you remember several things. A good frying pan is an essential—a nonstick or well-seasoned cast-iron one works best. Second, always add enough butter or oil to the pan so that the omelet will cook evenly and not stick. And third, make certain the temperature is hot enough so that the egg mixture will begin to set when poured into the pan, but not burn. Finally, you'll need to tilt the pan several times and lift up the edges of the eggs as they cook to let some of the uncooked mixture run underneath.

GRIDDLE SECRETS

Pancakes and Waffles

When combining the dry ingredients for pancake or waffle batters, it is important to whisk well so that the baking powder, in particular, is well distributed. When adding the dry ingredients to the liquid ones or vice versa, mix just until combined, but do not overbeat.

For pancakes, using either a griddle or large, heavy frying pan will yield griddle cakes that cook evenly and brown nicely. For medium-size griddle cakes, use a ¼-cup/60-ml ladle or measuring cup. Pancakes are ready to be turned when the bottoms are brown and bubbles appear on top. Cooked pancakes can be kept warm for a few minutes by placing them in a single layer on a heated platter and covering them loosely with foil.

For waffles, it's always a good idea to coat your waffle iron with nonstick spray even if it has a nonstick surface. Set it on the medium-high setting and follow the manufacturer's directions. For medium-size waffles, use a ½-cup/120-ml ladle or measuring cup. Keep cooked waffles warm by placing them on a baking sheet in a low oven until all the waffles are cooked.

BAKING NOTES FOR QUICK BREADS

- For muffins, scones, biscuits, popovers, and other quick breads, it's essential for the oven temperature to be as accurate as possible. Keep a thermometer in the oven to verify the temperature.
- Always give the oven plenty of time, usually about 20 minutes or longer, to preheat before baking.
- Eggs used in baking batters are best at room temperature.
- Use the type of flour called for in the recipe. The scones in this book are extra tender because they are made with cake flour rather than all-purpose flour.
- When baking muffins, grease the tins even if they are nonstick, or use paper liners.
- Be aware that baking times can vary slightly from those listed in the directions of a recipe.

EQUIPMENT ESSENTIALS

Brunch cookery does not require a lot of fancy equipment, but there are some basics that are helpful to have on hand. Consider the following a quick checklist.

For the Stove Top
- One medium and one large, heavy frying pan, preferably cast iron and/or nonstick
- One heavy griddle, if possible a large one that covers two burners

For the Oven
- Two large, heavy baking sheets, at least one that is rimmed
- Two standard and two mini-muffin tins, preferably nonstick
- Two 9-in/23-cm tart pans, one with a removable bottom
- One medium and one large oven-to-table baking dish
- Set of six 4- to 6-oz/115- to 170-g ramekins or custard cups

Useful Utensils
- Whisks, rubber spatulas (heat-resistant ones are particularly useful), and metal spatulas
- Stand or hand mixer

Special Equipment
- Waffle iron
- Popover pan
- Egg poacher pan

EGGS, EGGS, EGGS

Poached, Scrambled, Pan-Fried, and More

A long time ago when I was taking my first cooking classes, a student asked our talented Cordon Bleu–trained teacher what her favorite ingredients were. Without missing a beat, she reeled off a list and, not surprisingly, eggs were at the top. What she loved about them was their versatility.

When it comes to brunch, nothing is more popular or lends itself more readily to variation than eggs. You can poach, fry, scramble, and bake eggs, or turn them into omelets, all in only a few minutes time. The recipes in this chapter reflect wide-ranging choices. Beautiful poached eggs, with pillowy-soft whites and golden, runny yolks, are the basis for a New Orleans–inspired rendition of eggs Benedict. Another delectable entrée stars fried eggs, served sunny-side up, atop sautéed wild mushrooms and toasted sourdough slices. There's also a classic version of exceptionally creamy scrambled eggs along with several variations. Baked or shirred eggs are simplicity itself and can be enhanced, as they are here, with tempting garnishes like fresh crab and crème fraîche. For omelet lovers, you'll find three mouthwatering, distinctive fillings.

Whatever method you choose, always make an effort to buy the freshest eggs possible. Look for locally raised ones at farmers' markets; they often boast deep golden yolks due to the feed given the hens. If purchasing eggs at the supermarket, pick up the carton with the latest expiration date. Although I am partial to brown eggs (I like that rustic hue), whites work equally well. The choice is yours.

Eggs are the quintessential morning food and often the mainstay of brunches. The entries in this chapter should provide ample inspiration for making one of nature's most glorious foods into something extra special.

Poached Eggs, Asparagus, and Chorizo

Poached eggs set atop a mound of sleek asparagus spears, garnished with crispy bits of Spanish chorizo and toasted bread crumbs, make a simple yet impressive morning entrée. The sausage and bread crumbs contrast with the tender asparagus as well as with the soft eggs with their runny, sauce-like yolks.

Serves 4

PREP TIME:
15 minutes

START-TO-FINISH TIME:
45 minutes

MAKE AHEAD:
Partially

1½ tbsp olive oil

½ cup/30 g coarse fresh bread crumbs (see cooking tip)

4 oz/115 g Spanish chorizo cut into ½-in/ 12-mm cubes (use the Spanish-style chorizo in casing, not loose Mexican-style chorizo)

1¼ lb/680 g medium asparagus

Kosher salt

1 tbsp unsalted butter, diced

2 tsp fresh lemon juice

2 to 3 tbsp white or cider vinegar

4 eggs

Freshly ground black pepper

🥄 COOKING TIP:

To make bread crumbs, use a 1- to 2-day-old good-quality peasant or country bread with crusts removed. Process large chunks of it in a food processor to make coarse crumbs. Sourdough bread works particularly well.

1. Heat 1 tbsp of the olive oil until hot in a medium, heavy frying pan set over medium heat. Add the bread crumbs and cook, tossing constantly, until golden and crisp, 3 to 4 minutes. Remove the crumbs to a plate. (Crumbs can be prepared 1 hour ahead; cover and leave at room temperature.)

2. Heat the remaining ½ tbsp oil in the same frying pan set over medium heat. When hot, add the chorizo and stir until lightly browned, 3 minutes. Remove and set aside. (Chorizo can be prepared 1 hour ahead; leave at room temperature.)

3. Trim and discard 2 to 3 in/5 to 7.5 cm of the tough bases of the aparagus spears. Add the asparagus and 1 tsp salt to a large frying pan filled halfway with simmering water. Cook until the spears are just tender, 4 minutes. Drain and toss the asparagus in a large bowl with the butter and lemon juice. Season with salt and cover with foil.

4. Bring a large frying pan filled halfway with water to a boil. Add the vinegar and gently break each egg into a saucer and slide it into the water. Swirl the water with a wooden spoon while the eggs are cooking. Cook until the eggs are just set but the yolks are still soft, 3 minutes. Remove with a slotted spoon and drain well. (If you have an egg poacher, cook according to the manufacturer's directions until the eggs are set.)

5. Mound some asparagus spears on each of four dinner plates. Top each serving with a poached egg and sprinkle with the chorizo and bread crumbs. Season the eggs with several grinds of pepper and a pinch of salt and serve.

Eggs Benedict with New Orleans Accents

I spent my college years in New Orleans, where frequent trips for breakfast at Brennan's always included eggs Benedict. Theirs were prepared the traditional way with a toasted English muffin that was topped with Canadian bacon, a poached egg, and classic hollandaise. For a new version, I replaced the muffin with andouille-studded cornbread, and the bacon with sliced tomatoes. Of course, I included the anchor of this dish—a soft poached egg—and for the hollandaise I added a spicy accent of cayenne. I also made the sauce quickly in a processor rather than slowly at the stove.

Serves 4

PREP TIME:
15 minutes, plus
40 minutes to make
the cornbread

START-TO-FINISH TIME:
1 hour, including mak-
ing the cornbread

MAKE AHEAD:
Partially

Quick Hollandaise Sauce
½ cup/115 g unsalted butter, diced

3 egg yolks, at room temperature

1 tbsp fresh lemon juice

¼ tsp kosher salt

¼ to ½ tsp cayenne (more for a spicier accent)

Poached Eggs
2 to 3 tbsp cider or white vinegar

4 eggs

4 wedges Sausage-Studded Cornbread
  (page 77)

2 ripe tomatoes, sliced

Kosher salt

Freshly ground black pepper

Chopped chives or flat-leaf parsley, for garnish

COOKING TIP:

The cornbread recipe makes enough to serve 8.
If you want to double this recipe, it is easy to
make a double batch of hollandaise and poach
additional eggs.

1. For the Quick Hollandaise Sauce: Heat the butter in a small saucepan set over medium heat until foaming hot. Pour into a measuring cup with a spout. Place the egg yolks, lemon juice, salt, and cayenne in a food processor and process for 5 to 10 seconds to blend. Then, with the processor running, slowly add about 2 tbsp of the melted butter through the feed tube. (Most processors have a small hole in the bottom of the feed tube that will dispense liquids in a thin stream.) Repeat, adding 2 tbsp of butter at a time, until all has been incorporated and the sauce is thick and creamy. Pour the sauce into a heatproof bowl and place it in a shallow pan of barely simmering water.

2. For the poached eggs: Bring a large frying pan filled half-way with water to a boil. Add the vinegar and gently break each egg into a saucer and slide it into the water. Swirl the water with a wooden spoon while the eggs are cooking. Cook until the eggs are just set but the yolks are still soft, 3 minutes. Remove with a slotted spoon and drain well. (If you have an egg poacher, cook according to the manu-facturer's directions until eggs are set.)

3. Halve each cornbread wedge crosswise and arrange slightly overlapping on each of four dinner plates. Top the corn-bread with 2 or 3 tomato slices and then with a poached egg. Season with salt and pepper. Drizzle warm hollandaise over each, garnish with chives, and serve.

Best-Ever Scrambled Eggs

What makes these eggs different from the usual scrambled varieties are the little pieces of cream cheese that are stirred into the beaten mixture. When the eggs are cooked, these creamy morsels melt, imparting a smooth, silky texture to the finished dish. I've served these eggs countless times to guests, and without fail someone always comments on their creaminess.

Serves 4

PREP TIME:
5 minutes, or
10 minutes if doing
one of the variations

START-TO-FINISH TIME:
15 minutes, or
25 minutes if doing
one of the variations

MAKE AHEAD:
No

8 eggs

4 oz/115 g cream cheese at room temperature, cut into ½-in/12-mm pieces

1½ tbsp chopped flat-leaf parsley or chives

Kosher salt

Freshly ground black pepper

2½ tbsp unsalted butter

1. In a large bowl, whisk the eggs just to blend. Add the cream cheese and half of the parsley, and season with a pinch of salt and several grinds of pepper. Stir to mix.

2. Melt the butter in a large, nonstick frying pan set over medium heat. When butter has melted and is hot but not smoking, swirl it to cover the bottom of the pan and then add the egg mixture. With a wooden spoon or heat-resistant spatula, stir the eggs slowly until they just hold together and are cooked through, 2½ to 4 minutes. The eggs should still be moist and glistening.

3. Transfer to a serving platter and season with a few grinds of pepper. Sprinkle with the remaining parsley and serve.

VARIATIONS:

SMOKED TROUT, GREEN ONIONS, AND DILL
To the egg mixture, add 4 to 5 oz/115 to 140 g smoked trout (skin removed and flesh broken into small pieces) and ¼ cup/ 20 g chopped green onions. Replace the parsley with 1 tbsp fresh chopped dill. Cook as directed and, when done, garnish with ½ tbsp of additional chopped dill and a few grinds of pepper.

SAUSAGE AND THYME
Sauté 4 oz/115 g regular or turkey kielbasa or other mild, firm smoked sausage (cut into ½-in/12-mm pieces) in 1 tbsp melted butter in a large, nonstick frying pan over medium heat until lightly browned, 3 minutes. Add ¼ cup/20 g chopped green onions and 2 tsp dried thyme; cook 1 minute more. Remove to a plate and cool slightly.

To the egg mixture, add 1 tbsp coarse-grain mustard and omit the parsley. Stir in the sausage mixture. Cook as directed and, when done, garnish, if desired, with some fresh thyme sprigs.

Herbed Scrambled Eggs Nestled in Broiled Portobellos

The first time I served this dish at a brunch, my guests loved the look and taste of eggs seasoned with rosemary and set atop broiled portobello mushrooms. Although this entrée looks as if it might be difficult to prepare, it's actually quite easy. Extra-creamy scrambled eggs are mounded in each scooped-out mushroom cap and dusted with grated Parmesan.

Serves 6

PREP TIME:
20 minutes

START-TO-FINISH TIME:
40 minutes

MAKE AHEAD:
Partially

6 large portobello mushrooms, 4 to 5 in/
   10 to 12 cm in diameter
3 tbsp olive oil, plus more if needed
3 medium garlic cloves, minced
Kosher salt
Freshly ground black pepper
12 eggs
4 tbsp/30 g grated Parmesan cheese
1½ tsp minced fresh rosemary, plus
   6 rosemary sprigs for garnish
6 tbsp/85 g unsalted butter

1. Arrange a rack 4 to 5 in/10 to 12 cm from the broiler and preheat the broiler. Line a rimmed baking sheet with foil.

2. Remove and discard the mushroom stems. Scoop out and discard the tough inside centers where the stems were attached. Brush both sides of the mushrooms generously with the olive oil. Place the mushrooms, dark-gill-side up, on the prepared baking sheet. Sprinkle with the garlic, and then season generously with salt and pepper.

3. Broil the mushrooms until they begin to soften, 5 minutes. Then turn them over and broil until tender when pierced with a sharp knife, 7 minutes longer. (The mushrooms can be prepared 2 hours ahead. Leave at room temperature. Reheat in a preheated 350-degree-F/180-degree-C/gas-4 oven for about 10 minutes.)

4. In a large bowl, whisk together the eggs, 2 tbsp of the cheese, the minced rosemary, ¾ tsp salt, and ½ tsp pepper. Melt 5 tbsp/70 g of the butter in a large, nonstick frying pan set over medium heat. When the butter has melted and is hot but not smoking, swirl it to cover the bottom of the pan and then add the egg mixture. With a wooden spoon or heat-resistant spatula, stir the eggs slowly until they just hold together and are cooked through, 2½ to 4 minutes. The eggs should still be moist and glistening. Dot the eggs with the remaining 1 tbsp butter.

5. Serve the hot portobellos, gill-side up, on six plates. Divide the eggs evenly on top of the mushrooms and sprinkle with the remaining Parmesan and garnish with a rosemary sprig.

Pan-Fried Eggs and Mixed Mushroom Sauté on Toasted Sourdough Slices

This glorious egg dish calls for multitasking, so it's best served to a small group. However, with a little organization, you can streamline the cooking and dazzle everyone at the table. The mushrooms, which include both fresh and dried varieties, can be sautéed a day ahead and reheated at serving time. The bread slices can be quickly browned in a large frying pan and covered in foil. Finally, frying the eggs just until their yolks are soft and runny takes only about 3 minutes. All that is left then is a quick assembly.

Serves 4

PREP TIME:
25 minutes

START-TO-FINISH TIME:
50 minutes

MAKE AHEAD:
Partially

Mushroom Sauté
1¼ oz/35 g mixed dried mushrooms
    (see market note, page 26)
1½ cups/360 ml boiling water
3 tbsp olive oil
8 oz/225 g sliced brown mushrooms
2 tsp minced garlic
1 tsp dried crushed rosemary
    (see cooking tip, page 26)
Kosher salt
Freshly ground black pepper

Toast and Eggs
Four ½-in-/12-mm-thick sourdough slices,
    halved if the slices are extra large
Olive oil
2 tbsp unsalted butter
4 eggs
Kosher salt
Freshly ground black pepper
Rosemary sprigs for garnish, optional

1. For the Mushroom Sauté: Place the dried mushrooms in a medium bowl and cover with the boiling water. Let stand until softened, 20 minutes. Strain in a sieve lined with a double thickness of paper towels and reserve the soaking liquid. Coarsely chop the mushrooms.

2. Heat the olive oil in a medium, heavy frying pan set over medium heat. When hot, add the brown mushrooms and sauté, stirring often, for 6 minutes. Add the reserved mushrooms, garlic, rosemary, and ½ tsp salt; stir for 1 minute. Add the mushroom liquid and cook, stirring, until it has evaporated, 4 to 7 minutes. Season with salt and several grinds of pepper. Remove the frying pan from the heat and cover with foil to keep warm. (The mushrooms can be prepared 1 day ahead; cool, cover, and refrigerate. Reheat, stirring, over medium heat.)

3. For the toast and eggs: Brush both sides of the bread slices generously with olive oil. Set a 10- to 11-in/25- to 28-cm nonstick frying pan over medium-high heat, and, when hot, add the bread and cook until lightly browned, about 2 minutes per side. Remove the toast and cover loosely with foil. When pan is cool enough to handle, wipe it out with clean paper towels.

continued . . .

4. Add the butter to the frying pan and set it over medium heat. When the butter starts to foam, break an egg into a saucer, being careful to remove any shell fragments, and gently slide it into the frying pan. Repeat with the remaining eggs. Immediately reduce the heat to low and cook, basting the eggs with some of the butter in the pan frequently, until the whites are firm and the yolks are still soft and runny, 3 minutes.

5. While the eggs are cooking, arrange a toasted bread slice on each of four plates. Mound the mushrooms evenly over the toast.

6. Remove each egg with a spatula and arrange on top of the mushrooms. Season with salt and pepper and, if desired, garnish each serving with a rosemary sprig. Serve immediately.

 MARKET NOTE:

Whole Foods sells a nice blend of mixed dried mushrooms. If unavailable, you can use all dried porcini.

 COOKING TIP:

If you can't find dried crushed rosemary, crush regular dried rosemary in an electric spice mill, or place it in a self-sealing plastic bag and roll over it with a rolling pin.

Eggs Baked with Crème Fraîche, Crab, and Tarragon

In a small Paris café one warm summer day, I ordered an "oeuf en cocotte au crabe et l'estragon," which translates as "an egg in a dish with crab and tarragon." I wasn't sure what to expect, but after my first bite, I was in heaven. The chef had baked an egg in a small gratin pan, and then topped it with fresh crab, crème fraîche, and a sprinkling of fresh tarragon. This dish included only four major ingredients, but they were magical together. A basket of lightly toasted country bread accompanied my "oeuf," and I used it to sop up the delicious residue in the pan.

Serves 4

PREP TIME:
10 minutes

START-TO-FINISH TIME:
20 minutes

MAKE AHEAD:
No

½ cup/120 ml crème fraîche

½ tbsp unsalted butter

4 eggs, preferably large or extra large

Kosher salt

Freshly ground black pepper

4 oz/115 g fresh crabmeat, picked over and brought to room temperature for 30 minutes (see market note)

4 tsp chopped fresh tarragon

EQUIPMENT NEEDED:

Four crème brûlée or four small individual gratin dishes, about 5 in/12 cm in diameter.

COOKING TIP:

Crème fraîche, a thick cream used in French cooking, is available in the dairy section of many supermarkets.

MARKET NOTE:

The success of this dish depends on using fresh crabmeat. Canned pasteurized crab will not produce the same bright flavor.

1. Arrange a rack at center position and preheat the oven to 350 degrees F/180 degrees C/gas 4.

2. Place the crème fraîche in a small saucepan and set over low heat just to liquefy, 1 minute or less. Set aside.

3. Generously butter the baking dishes. Break an egg into each dish, and then place the dishes on the center rack and bake until the white of each egg is firm and the yolk is thickened (but still runny), 8 to 12 minutes. Start checking the eggs at 8 minutes. Watch carefully and, when done, remove from the oven. (Note: Although the eggs are cooked in this recipe, the yolks are still soft. Children, the elderly, or those with immune deficiencies might want to avoid eggs with yolks that are slightly undercooked.)

4. Season each egg with salt and pepper. Sprinkle some fresh crab in a ring around each yolk, and then spoon 2 tbsp crème fraîche over the crab. Garnish each with a sprinkle of tarragon. Serve immediately.

Potato and Arugula Omelets

Sautéed diced potatoes, some grated Gruyère, and an abundance of coarsely chopped arugula combine to make a nutty and peppery filling for omelets. Since the arugula is cooked only a few seconds, it retains its bright green hue and adds a bit of texture. Have all the ingredients for the filling ready before you start to make the omelets, and then count on less than 5 minutes from start to finish for each one. And try the variations!

Serves 2

PREP TIME:
15 minutes (Time is about the same for variations)

START-TO-FINISH TIME:
35 minutes

MAKE AHEAD:
No

2½ tbsp unsalted butter

½ tbsp olive oil

4 oz/115 g red-skinned potatoes, scrubbed but not peeled, cut into ½-in/12-mm cubes

Kosher salt

Freshly ground black pepper

4 eggs

⅛ tsp cayenne pepper

8 cups/120 g arugula, stems discarded and leaves cleaned, dried, and coarsely chopped (see market note, page 30)

½ tbsp balsamic vinegar

6 tbsp/30 g grated Gruyère cheese

1. Heat ½ tbsp of the butter and the olive oil in a medium, heavy frying pan set over medium heat. When hot, add the potatoes and sauté, stirring often, until light golden and tender, 8 minutes. Remove from the heat and season with salt and pepper. (The potatoes can be prepared 1 hour ahead; leave at room temperature. Reheat, stirring, over medium heat.)

2. Whisk the eggs in a mixing bowl and season with a good pinch of salt and the cayenne. Place the arugula in another mixing bowl and toss with the vinegar. Place the Gruyère and the potatoes each in separate bowls. Have ready a ladle for adding the egg mixture to the pan.

3. Add 1 tbsp butter to a 9-in/23-cm frying pan, preferably nonstick or seasoned cast iron, set over medium heat. Swirl the butter so that it coats the bottom of the pan. When it is hot but not smoking, ladle half of the eggs into the pan and stir with the back of a fork until they start to set but are still quite liquid on the top, 30 to 40 seconds. With the fork or a nonstick spatula, lift an edge of the omelet and tilt the pan to let some of the uncooked egg mixture run underneath. Repeat this two or three more times, working your way around the pan until the eggs are cooked but remain moist on top.

continued . . .

4. Sprinkle half of the potatoes, then half of the cheese, and finally half of the arugula over the eggs. Let the mixture cook until the cheese begins to melt and the arugula wilts only slightly, 30 seconds. Using a nonstick or metal spatula, fold the omelet in half and slide it onto a plate. Repeat to make another omelet.

5. Serve each omelet as soon as it is prepared (see cooking tip).

 MARKET NOTE:

You can use regular or baby arugula, but the former provides a more intense flavor.

 COOKING TIP:

If you are increasing this recipe and want to serve everyone at the same time, you can slide the finished omelets onto a baking sheet and keep them warm in a low (200 degrees F/ 95 degrees C) oven until all are finished. However, I prefer to serve each omelet as it is done, and no one ever seems to mind waiting a few minutes for his or her turn.

TWO OTHER OMELET FILLING VARIATIONS

Each variation makes enough for 2 omelets

ASPARAGUS, MUSHROOM, AND FONTINA

½ lb/225 g medium asparagus, tough ends discarded, cut into
  1-in/2.5-cm pieces
Kosher salt
3 tbsp olive oil
¼ lb/115 g thinly sliced white or brown mushrooms
½ tsp dried crushed rosemary (see cooking tip, page 26)
6 tbsp/35 g grated fontina cheese

1. Blanch the asparagus in boiling, salted water to cover, until just tender, 3 to 4 minutes. Drain and pat dry.

2. Heat the olive oil in a medium frying pan over medium heat. When hot, sauté the mushrooms, stirring, until browned, 6 minutes. Stir in the asparagus and rosemary; cook 1 minute more and season with salt.

3. Cook as directed, using half of this mixture as a filling for each omelet along with half the fontina.

TOMATO, GOAT CHEESE, AND MINT

4 oz/115 g tomatoes, unpeeled, seeded, and cut into ½-in/12-mm dice
4 medium green onions, including 2 in/5 cm of green stems, chopped
2 tbsp chopped fresh mint
Kosher salt
6 tbsp/60 g creamy goat cheese, broken into small pieces

1. Combine the tomatoes, green onions, and mint in a bowl; season lightly with salt.

2. Cook as directed, using half of this mixture as a filling for each omelet along with a sprinkle of half of the goat cheese.

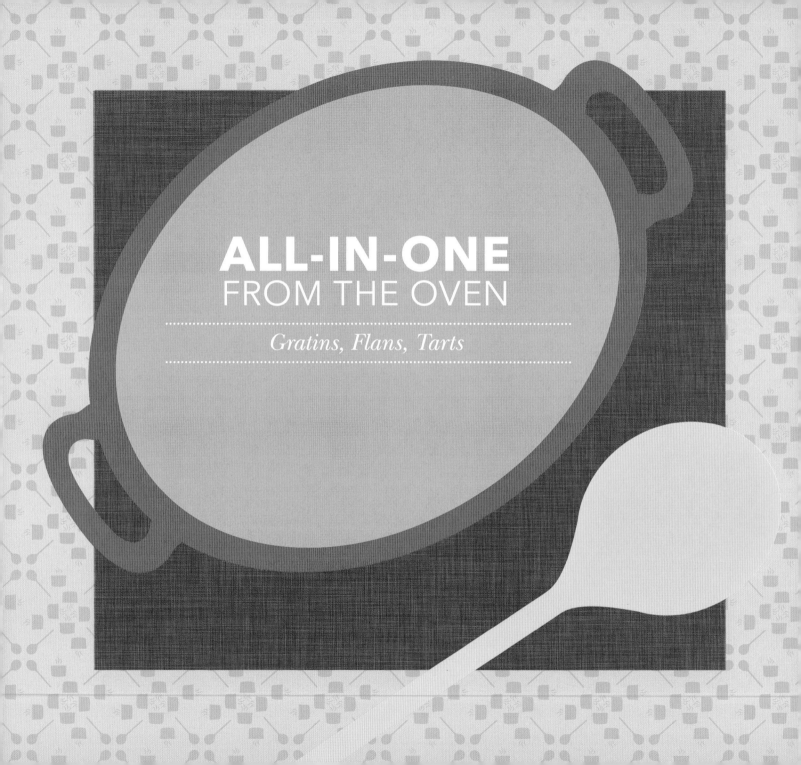

ALL-IN-ONE
FROM THE OVEN

Gratins, Flans, Tarts

You could call the recipes in this chapter a brunch cook's "dream dishes," since each is easily an all-in-one main course. Rich and satisfying, these entrees take leading roles in a meal and need only simple accompaniments. The recipes include tarts—both an impressive standard-size one as well as individual tartlets—and savory flans, prepared with the usual eggs and cream but enriched with enticing additions, such as Parmesan cheese. Stratas, those popular dishes of the past in which beaten egg mixtures are poured over cubes of toasted bread, are given visual and palate-tempting updates. You'll also discover savory gratins with tempting flavors.

Some of these one-dish wonders are vegetarian, like the Grape Tomato and Blue Cheese Tart, and the Parmesan Flans with Parmesan Crisps. Others get flavor boosts from shellfish, bacon, or ham. A few would be perfect for holiday celebrations. Try the Spicy Shrimp and Grits for Mardi Gras fetes, and the Gratin of Eggs, Leeks, Bacon, and St. André Cheese, which can be assembled the night before, on Christmas morning.

Serve these scrumptious brunch entrees with a salad of your favorite greens, plus some fresh seasonal fruit or one of the fruit creations from the Fruits for all Seasons chapter, and you've got a winning menu.

Gratin of Eggs, Leeks, Bacon, and St. André Cheese

This dish can be assembled the night before, put in the fridge, and popped into the oven the next morning. Toasted French bread, sautéed leeks, crispy fried bacon, and bits of creamy St. André are all combined with a savory mixture of eggs and half-and-half. Since this entree includes the classic breakfast trilogy—bacon, eggs, and toast—you only need to add some fresh fruit to round out the menu.

Serves 6

PREP TIME:
20 minutes

START-TO-FINISH TIME:
2 hours, 15 minutes; including 1 hour for the gratin to rest

MAKE AHEAD:
Partially

Unsalted butter, for the baking dish

1 baguette, about 2½ to 3 in/6 to 7.5 cm in diameter

6 thick slices (about 6 oz/170 g) bacon, cut into 1-in/2.5-cm pieces

2 cups/160 g chopped leeks, white and light green parts (about 4 leeks)

6 oz/170 g St. André cheese, well chilled (see market note, page 36)

6 eggs

2½ cups/600 ml half-and-half

½ tsp salt

Generous 2 pinches of cayenne pepper

1 tbsp minced flat-leaf parsley or chives

1. Arrange a rack at center position and preheat the oven to 350 degrees F/180 degrees C/gas 4. Generously butter a 9-by-13-in/23-by-33-cm baking dish.

2. Cut enough ½-in-/12-mm-thick slices from the baguette to make a single layer in the baking dish. (You'll probably need between 20 and 24 slices; save any extra slices for another use.) Arrange the slices on a baking sheet and bake without turning until crisp and very lightly colored, 10 minutes. Remove and arrange the slices in the baking dish.

3. In a medium, heavy frying pan set over medium heat, fry the bacon pieces until crisp and browned, 5 minutes. Drain on paper towels.

4. Pour off all but 1 tbsp of the drippings and return the frying pan to medium heat. Add the leeks and cook, stirring, until just softened, 4 to 5 minutes. Sprinkle the leeks and bacon over the bread slices in the baking dish.

continued . . .

5. Cut the St. André with its rind into ½-in/12-mm cubes and scatter them over the leeks and bacon in the baking dish. In a medium bowl, whisk the eggs to blend, and then whisk in the half-and-half, salt, and cayenne. Pour the mixture into the baking dish. Let the gratin stand at least 1 hour, or cover the pan with plastic wrap and refrigerate for up to 24 hours. (If the dish has been refrigerated, let it stand at room temperature for 30 minutes before baking if you have time. It also can go directly from the refrigerator to the oven but will take longer to cook.)

6. Bake the gratin until the egg mixture is set, the top is golden, and the mixture is bubbly, 40 to 45 minutes (10 to 15 minutes longer if straight from the refrigerator). Remove and let cool for about 5 minutes. Sprinkle with the minced parsley and serve hot.

 MARKET NOTE:

St. André cheese is a mild, triple-cream French cheese with a white rind. It is available at many grocers and cheese stores. If you are unable to find it, you can substitute a triple-cream Brie.

Souffléd Eggs with Ricotta, Spinach, and Pancetta

Simple to prepare, this delectable strata makes a striking presentation when it comes out of the oven. A custard base of eggs, cream, and ricotta is combined with chopped spinach and sautéed pancetta and then poured over toasted bread cubes. When baked, the eggs puff up, soufflé-style, and rise just slightly above the edges of the baking pan. The golden gratin looks especially tempting flecked with bits of spinach.

Serves 5 to 6

PREP TIME:
20 minutes

START-TO-FINISH TIME:
1 hour

MAKE AHEAD:
No

Unsalted butter, for the baking dish

2 oz/55 g day-old baguette, crusts removed, cut into ½-in/12-mm or smaller cubes

1 to 1½ tbsp olive oil

8 eggs

1 cup/240 ml heavy cream

½ cup/120 ml whole milk ricotta

½ tsp freshly grated nutmeg

¼ tsp kosher salt

Generous pinch of cayenne pepper

2 grinds fresh black pepper

1½ cups/60 g coarsely chopped baby spinach leaves

4 oz/115 g pancetta, cut into ¼-in/6-mm cubes, fried until crisp

1. Arrange a rack at center position and preheat the oven to 375 degrees F/190 degree C/gas 5. Generously butter a 1½-qt/1.4-L shallow oven-to-table baking dish.

2. Place the bread cubes in a medium bowl and toss with enough olive oil to coat lightly. Spread the bread cubes on a baking sheet and bake until just golden, 5 minutes. Remove and spread in the bottom of the prepared baking dish.

3. In a large mixing bowl, whisk the eggs until blended. Then whisk in the cream, ricotta, nutmeg, salt, cayenne, and pepper just to blend. Stir in the spinach and pancetta. Pour the mixture over the toasted bread.

4. Bake until the egg mixture puffs up (soufflé-like) and a knife inserted into the center comes out clean, 30 to 40 minutes. Remove from the oven and cool 5 minutes before serving.

Parmesan Flans with Parmesan Crisps

Served in individual ramekins with a Parmesan crisp, these delectable flans make a unforgettable entree for mid-morning menus. The eggs, crème fraîche, and half-and-half give these savory custards their silken texture, while rosemary, grated Parmesan, and a pinch of cayenne pepper provide subtle but distinctive flavorings. The flans can be served as soon as they come out of the oven, or cooked a day ahead and reheated when needed. These flans, served in their ramekins, do not need to be unmolded—a definite bonus for busy cooks.

Serves 6

PREP TIME:
10 minutes for the flans and 5 minutes for the crisps

START-TO-FINISH TIME:
50 minutes

MAKE AHEAD:
Yes

Unsalted butter, for the ramekins

4 eggs

1 cup/240 ml crème fraîche (see cooking tip, page 27)

1½ cups/360 ml half-and-half

¾ cup/90 g coarsely grated Parmesan cheese

¼ tsp dried crushed rosemary (see cooking tip, page 26)

¼ tsp kosher salt

Very generous pinch of cayenne pepper

Parmesan Crisps (page 40)

6 fresh rosemary sprigs

1. Arrange a rack at center position and preheat the oven to 350 degrees F/180 degrees C/gas 4. Butter six ½-cup/120-ml ramekins, soufflé dishes, or custard cups. Place the ramekins in a baking pan large enough to hold them in a single layer.

2. In a bowl, whisk together the eggs, crème fraîche, half-and-half, Parmesan, rosemary, salt, and cayenne until well mixed. Transfer to a 4-cup/960-ml or larger measuring cup with a spout and pour it into the ramekins, filling them almost to the top.

3. Pour enough hot water into the baking pan to come halfway up the sides of the ramekins. Carefully place the pan in the oven. Bake until the flans are set and a small, sharp knife or tester inserted into the centers comes out clean, 35 to 40 minutes. Using pot holders, remove the ramekins from the pan to a cooling rack for 5 minutes. (The flans can be prepared 1 day ahead. Cool, cover with plastic wrap, and refrigerate. Bring to room temperature and reheat, uncovered, on a baking sheet in a preheated 350-degree-F/180-degree-C/gas-4 oven, for 15 minutes.)

4. Place a flan on each of six salad plates. Tuck a crisp upright into the center of each flan, garnish with a rosemary sprig, and serve.

PARMESAN CRISPS

These golden little cheese crisps take only minutes to assemble and cook. The key to their success lies in using a nonstick pan, getting the temperature correct, and letting them stand a few seconds before turning them over. They can be prepared ahead, so no last-minute fuss is necessary.

Makes 6 to 7 crisps

½ cup/60 g very finely grated Parmesan cheese (see market note)

1½ tsp all-purpose flour

¼ tsp dried crushed rosemary (see cooking tip, page 26)

Pinch of cayenne pepper

 MARKET NOTE:

Finely grated Parmesan cheese (powder-like in consistency) is available in most supermarkets and works beautifully in this recipe.

1. In a small bowl, stir together the Parmesan, flour, rosemary, and cayenne. Place a medium, nonstick frying pan over medium heat and heat until it is hot enough to make a drop of water sizzle.

2. Spoon 1 tbsp of the cheese mixture into the pan. With the back of a spoon, flatten the mixture into an even thin layer, as close to a circle as possible. Repeat to make one or two more crisps, and then reduce the heat to low. Cook until the cheese melts, bubbles, and begins to turn golden, 1 to 1½ minutes.

3. Remove the pan from the heat and let the crisps rest for 30 to 40 seconds to firm. Using a heatproof spatula, carefully loosen the crisps and turn them over. Let stand for 30 seconds more on the other side. Remove the crisps to a plate. Repeat with the remaining cheese mixture. Cool completely, then store for up to 1 day in a self-sealing plastic bag at room temperature.

Caramelized Shallot and Ham Tartlets

These tarts, which can be prepared several hours ahead, need only about 20 minutes to bake to a golden flakiness and are best served hot. As the tarts bake, the sides rise up magically to surround the savory filling. A single recipe yields four generous servings, but can easily be doubled for larger gatherings.

Serves 4

PREP TIME:
20 minutes

START-TO-FINISH TIME:
1 hour

MAKE AHEAD:
Partially

1½ tbsp unsalted butter, plus more for the baking sheet

¾ lb/340 g shallots

1½ tbsp canola oil

4 oz/115 g good-quality diced ham, cut into ¼-in/6-mm dice

½ tsp dried thyme

Kosher salt

Freshly ground black pepper

1 sheet puff pastry from a 17.3-oz/490-g package, defrosted (see market note)

Flour for work surface

3 tsp Dijon mustard

1 to 2 oz/30 to 55 g shaved Gruyère cheese

 MARKET NOTE:

A 17.3-oz/490 g package of Pepperidge Farm puff pastry contains two sheets, each about 9 in/23 cm square. Defrost according to the package directions in the fridge, and keep refrigerated until ready to use.

1. Butter a large, heavy baking sheet and set aside.

2. Halve the shallots lengthwise, trim and discard the ends, and then remove the peel. Cut the shallots crosswise into ½-in-/12-mm-thick slices. Melt the 1½ tbsp butter and the canola oil in a large, heavy frying pan set over medium heat. Add the shallots and reduce the heat to medium-low. Cook, stirring frequently to break apart the slices, until lightly browned, about 12 minutes; do not overcook. Stir in the ham and thyme. Season lightly with salt and several grinds of pepper. Cool to room temperature.

3. Place the puff pastry sheet on a lightly floured work surface and, using a rolling pin, gently flatten the seams. Cut the sheet into four equal squares. Using a sharp knife, gently trace a ¾-in/2-cm border inside each pastry square, taking care not to cut all the way through the dough. Transfer the squares to a baking sheet and refrigerate for 10 minutes.

4. Brush the area within the traced lines of each square with ¾ tsp mustard, and then divide the shallot mixture evenly and spoon inside the traced lines. (The tartlets can be prepared 2 hours ahead; cover and refrigerate.)

5. When ready to bake the tartlets, arrange a rack at center position and preheat the oven to 400 degrees F/200 degrees C/gas 6. Bake the tartlets for 15 minutes, and then remove from the oven and sprinkle the top of each with the Gruyère. Bake until the sides have puffed and are golden brown and the cheese has melted, about 5 minutes. Serve hot.

Grape Tomato and Blue Cheese Tart

With its flaky crust and delectable topping of sweet grape tomatoes and creamy blue cheese, this tart makes an enticing vegetarian dish for brunch. The exceptionally crispy pastry shell is prepared with cream cheese and seasoned generously with cayenne pepper. The tart can be baked several hours ahead, left at room temperature, and then quickly reheated.

Serves 6

PREP TIME:
20 minutes

START-TO-FINISH TIME:
1 hour, 30 minutes

MAKE AHEAD:
Yes

Crust

1 cup/115 g all-purpose flour

4 oz/115 g cream cheese, chilled and cut into ½-in/12-mm pieces

8 tbsp/115 g unsalted butter, chilled and cut into ½-in/12-mm pieces

¼ tsp salt

⅛ tsp cayenne pepper

Topping

4 oz/115 g creamy blue cheese (such as Bleu d'Auvergne), finely crumbled

2 cups/298 g grape tomatoes, halved lengthwise (see market note)

2 tsp olive oil

1 tsp balsamic vinegar

Kosher salt

1½ tbsp chopped flat-leaf parsley

2 green onions, chopped to include 2 in/5 cm of the green parts

MARKET NOTE:

Small grape tomatoes, which have a sweet flavor, work better than larger cherry tomatoes in this recipe, and can be used year-round. However, in the summer feel free to try the tart with one of your favorite varieties. Sweet ones that are on the small side work best.

1. Arrange a rack at center position and preheat the oven to 375 degrees F/190 degrees C/gas 5. Have ready a 9-in/23-cm tart pan with a removable bottom.

2. For the crust: Place the flour, cream cheese, butter, salt, and cayenne in a food processor; pulse until the mixture resembles coarse meal. Remove and knead the mixture into a smooth mass, and then press it with your fingers in an even layer into the bottom (not up the sides) of the tart pan. Smooth the dough with the back of a spoon. Freeze the tart shell for 15 minutes to firm, and then bake the crust until golden brown, 30 minutes. Remove the tart shell from the oven and cool for about 5 minutes but retain oven temperature.

3. For the topping: Sprinkle the cheese evenly over the crust. Arrange the tomatoes in a circular pattern and in a single layer over the cheese, cut-sides up. You may not need to use all of the tomatoes. Whisk together the olive oil and vinegar and drizzle over the tomatoes, and then sprinkle with salt. Place the tart on a baking sheet to catch any drippings and return to the oven and bake until the cheese has melted and the tomatoes are hot, 10 to 12 minutes.

4. Cool the tart for 5 to 10 minutes and then remove the sides of the tart pan. (The tart can be made 3 hours ahead. Leave the tart at cool room temperature and reheat in a preheated 350-degree-F/180-degree-C/gas-4 oven until warmed through, 8 to 10 minutes.)

5. Mix together the parsley and green onions, and sprinkle over the tart. Cut the tart into six wedges and serve.

Spicy Shrimp and Grits

From the first bite, I knew that these extra-creamy grits, seasoned with a duo of cheeses and topped with tomatoes, shrimp, and andouille sausage, were redolent of New Orleans. This Louisiana-inspired dish is a great choice for a weekend brunch, especially around Mardi Gras. The grits, which can be assembled a day ahead, need only about a half hour in the oven. That leaves you with plenty of time to prepare the colorful shrimp and sausage topping. A warm, crusty baguette and a mixed green salad would make fine partners to this delicious main course.

Serves 6

PREP TIME:
1 hour, including
making the grits

START-TO-FINISH TIME:
1 hour, 5 minutes

MAKE AHEAD:
Partially

Spicy Shrimp
1 tbsp olive oil
6 oz/170 g andouille sausage, cut into
⅟₂-in/12-mm dice
⅓ cup/30 g chopped green onion (including
2 in/5 cm of green parts)
2 tsp minced garlic
One 14-oz/400-g can diced tomatoes,
drained well
⅛ tsp cayenne pepper, plus more if needed
1 lb/455 g medium shrimp (30-count), peeled
and deveined with tails left on
Kosher salt
Freshly ground black pepper

Southern Cheese Grits (page 96)
1½ tbsp chopped flat-leaf parsley

1. To prepare the Spicy Shrimp: Heat the olive oil in a large, heavy frying pan set over medium heat. When hot, add the sausage and cook, stirring, until lightly browned, 3 minutes. Add the green onions and garlic and stir for 1 minute. Add the tomatoes and cayenne and stir for 2 minutes more. Finally, add the shrimp and cook, stirring, until they turn pink and curl, 4 to 5 minutes (do not overcook). Season with salt and pepper. (For a spicier taste, add additional cayenne.)

2. Place the grits on each of six plates. Spoon the shrimp mixture down the center of the grits. Sprinkle the chopped parsley over the shrimp and serve.

HOT OFF THE GRIDDLE

Pancakes, Waffles, French Toast

Of all the brunch choices possible, nothing is more tempting than that triumvirate of griddle specialties—pancakes, waffles, and French toast. Grown-ups love these foods because they revive memories of their family's special waffle recipe, or the first French toast or pancakes they helped prepare. Kids today are just as crazy about these timeless favorites. Ever since they could stand on kitchen stools to reach the counter, my own grandchildren have been my enthusiastic assistants when I make griddle cakes.

A host of classics are included in this chapter, most with new twists to add an extra dimension of flavor. There are boldly spiced flapjacks served with maple-butter syrup, as well as light-as-air ricotta pancakes topped with thick, cinnamon-scented blueberry sauce. Pecan-studded waffles, partnered with warm salted caramel sauce and bananas, are hard to resist. Equally tempting is French toast, soaked in eggnog, baked in the oven, and then crowned with glazed cranberries and apples. These dishes are all easy and impressive at the same time.

Nestled among these favorites is a recipe for blini—those savory little Russian pancakes served with toppings of sour cream, caviar, and smoked fish. Bite-size and addictive, they are best served as appetizers, rather than as a main course like their sweet counterparts.

Savory or sweet, griddled fare is a universal crowd-pleaser. One little caveat applies: Make more rather than less. I've seen platters of pancakes and waffles disappear in minutes. People seem to eat with abandon, reaching for seconds and even thirds when the food is hot off the griddle.

10-Minute Blini

Classic Russian blini are prepared with buckwheat flour and yeast. In this version, whole-wheat flour replaces the heavy and strongly flavored buckwheat, while baking powder stands in for the yeast. By eliminating the yeast, the batter takes only about 10 minutes to put together. Sour cream and caviar are timeless toppings for these savory little pancakes, but other garnishes such as smoked salmon or trout, red onions, and lemon zest are just as delectable. These bite-size griddle cakes are blank canvases awaiting your artistic expression and make mouthwatering openers for a brunch.

Makes 12 blini, to serve 4

PREP TIME:
10 minutes

START-TO-FINISH TIME:
20 minutes

MAKE AHEAD:
No

½ cup/85 g whole-wheat flour

⅜ tsp baking powder

⅛ tsp baking soda

⅛ tsp salt

⅓ cup/75 ml sour cream

¼ cup/60 ml whole milk

1 egg

2 to 3 tbsp unsalted butter, plus more if needed

Toppings

Sour cream and caviar (either black or red)

Thinly sliced smoked salmon, finely chopped red onion, sour cream, a sprinkle of lemon zest, and several grinds of black pepper

Watercress sprig, thinly sliced apple, flaked smoked trout, sour cream mixed with a little horseradish, and a sprinkle of fleur de sel

1. Arrange a rack at center position and preheat the oven to 200 degrees F/95 degrees C. Have ready a baking sheet.

2. In a medium bowl, whisk together the flour, baking powder, baking soda, and salt. In another medium bowl, whisk together the sour cream, milk, and egg until just blended. Gradually pour the sour cream mixture into the dry ingredients, whisking until the mixture is thick and smooth.

3. Place a large, heavy frying pan or griddle over medium-low heat and add enough butter to coat the bottom of the pan. When the butter is hot but not smoking, add the batter in level tablespoonfuls. Add just enough to fit comfortably in the pan, and cook until the blini are golden brown on the bottom, 1½ to 2 minutes. Turn and cook until golden brown on the other side, 1½ to 2 minutes more. Remove to the baking sheet and place in the oven to keep warm. Repeat, adding more butter to the pan as needed until all the batter has been used.

4. Arrange the blini on a serving plate, garnish with any of the suggested toppings, and serve.

Spiced Pancakes with Warm Maple-Butter Syrup

Made with a classic batter of flour, eggs, sugar, and butter that is enhanced by a quartet of fragrant spices, these golden pancakes are topped with a drizzle of Warm Maple-Butter Syrup. The recipe yields four servings, but can be easily doubled. The delectable syrup can be prepared ahead and the dry ingredients combined in advance, so that last-minute prep is kept to a minimum.

Makes 12 pancakes, to serve 4

PREP TIME:
15 minutes, including making the Warm Maple-Butter Syrup

START-TO-FINISH TIME:
25 minutes

MAKE AHEAD:
Partially

Warm Maple-Butter Syrup

6 tbsp/85 g unsalted butter, diced

6 tbsp/90 ml maple syrup

Pancakes

1½ cups/175 g all-purpose flour

3 tbsp granulated sugar

1 tbsp baking powder

1 tsp cinnamon

½ tsp ground ginger

¼ tsp salt

⅛ tsp ground cloves

⅛ tsp freshly ground nutmeg

1 cup/240 ml whole milk

3 eggs, beaten

4 tbsp/55 g unsalted butter, melted, plus more for the griddle

Confectioners' sugar, for garnish

COOKING TIP

Dry ingredients can be assembled a day ahead; cover and store at room temperature.

1. For the Warm Maple-Butter Syrup: Place the butter and maple syrup in a small, heavy saucepan set over medium heat. Heat, stirring, until the butter has melted and blended with the syrup, 1 to 2 minutes. (This mixture can be prepared 2 hours ahead; leave at room temperature and reheat, stirring, over medium heat.) Pour into a heat-proof pitcher, such as a small creamer. Rub the underside of the lip of the pitcher with a dab of butter to prevent dribbles.

2. For the pancakes: In a large bowl, whisk together the flour, granulated sugar, baking powder, cinnamon, ginger, salt, cloves, and nutmeg. In another bowl, whisk together the milk, eggs, and melted butter. Pour the liquid ingredients into the dry ones, and whisk to combine.

3. Heat a griddle or a large, heavy frying pan set over medium heat until hot, and then brush with just enough butter to coat the surface. Working in batches, pour generous ¼ cup/60 ml measures of the batter onto the hot griddle. Cook until bubbles appear on the tops and the pancakes are golden brown on the bottom, 1 to 2 minutes. Turn and cook until golden brown on the other side, about 2 minutes. Remove to a warm platter, and cover loosely with foil. (Do not stack the pancakes or they will steam and become flabby.) Repeat, adding more butter to the griddle until all the batter has been used.

4. Arrange three overlapping pancakes on each of four plates, and drizzle with some of the warm syrup. Dust with confectioners' sugar and serve.

Lemon-Ricotta Pancakes with Blueberry Sauce

Ricotta cheese gives these golden pancakes their rich, smooth texture, while a generous addition of lemon zest provides a refreshing citrus accent. Beaten egg whites contribute a light airiness to the batter. The scrumptious blueberry sauce that accompanies these griddle cakes is simple to assemble, but needs a little simmering time to concentrate the flavors. You can make the sauce three days ahead and reheat it at serving time.

Makes 12 pancakes, to serve 4

PREP TIME:
45 minutes, including making the blueberry sauce

START-TO-FINISH TIME:
1 hour

MAKE AHEAD:
Partially

Blueberry Sauce

1 cup/240 ml cold water

½ cup/100 g sugar

3 tbsp fresh lemon juice

2 tbsp cornstarch

2 cups/280 g fresh or frozen unsweetened blueberries (defrosted and patted dry)

⅛ tsp ground cinnamon

Pancakes

⅔ cup/80 g all-purpose flour

½ tsp baking powder

¼ tsp salt

2 eggs, separated

1 cup/225 g whole milk ricotta cheese

½ cup/240 ml whole milk

2 tbsp sugar

2 tbsp grated lemon zest

Canola oil

1. For the Blueberry Sauce: Combine the water, sugar, lemon juice, and cornstarch in a heavy, medium saucepan and stir until blended. Place the pan over low heat and cook, stirring, until the cornstarch dissolves. Add the blueberries and raise the heat to medium. Cook, stirring, until the sauce thickens and coats the back of a spoon, about 5 minutes. Remove and let cool for about 10 minutes.

2. Purée the sauce in a food processor or blender until smooth. Strain the puréed sauce through a fine-meshed sieve back into the saucepan. Return to medium heat and cook at a simmer until reduced to 1 cup/240 ml, about 30 minutes. Stir in the cinnamon. (The sauce can be prepared 3 days ahead; cool, cover, and refrigerate. Reheat over low heat when needed.)

3. For the pancakes: In a medium bowl, whisk together the flour, baking powder, and salt. In a large bowl, whisk together the egg yolks, ricotta, milk, sugar, and lemon zest until well blended. Gradually whisk in the dry ingredients.

continued . . .

4. With an electric mixer on medium-high speed, beat the egg whites until they are just firm. Gently stir one-third of the whites into the batter to lighten it. Then gently fold in the remaining egg whites.

5. Heat a griddle or a large, heavy frying pan set over medium to medium-low heat until hot, and then brush with just enough canola oil to coat the surface. Working in batches, pour generous ¼ cup/60 ml measures of the batter onto the hot griddle. Cook until bubbles appear on the tops and the pancakes are golden brown on the bottom, 1 to 2 minutes. Turn and cook until golden brown on the other side, about 2 minutes. Remove to a warm platter, and cover loosely with foil. (Do not stack the pancakes or they will steam and become flabby.) Repeat, adding more oil to the griddle until all the batter has been used.

6. Arrange three overlapping pancakes on each of four plates, drizzle with some of the warm blueberry sauce, and serve.

Golden Pecan Waffles with Warm Salted Caramel Sauce and Bananas

Crispy, golden, and studded with pecans, these waffles, which are lightly sweetened, are a perfect foil for a rich dark caramel sauce with bananas. A touch of fleur de sel intensifies the flavor of the sauce, which can be prepared two days ahead.

Makes about six 6½-in/16.5-cm waffles; serves 4 to 6

PREP TIME:
25 minutes, including making the caramel sauce

START-TO-FINISH TIME:
45 minutes

MAKE AHEAD:
Partially

Warm Salted Caramel Sauce

1½ cups/300 g sugar

¾ cup/180 ml water

⅔ cup/165 ml half-and-half

4 tbsp/55 g unsalted butter, diced

½ tsp fleur de sel

3 ripe, but not soft, bananas, cut into
   ½-in/12-mm slices

Golden Pecan Waffles

1¾ cups/225 g all-purpose flour

4 tsp sugar

2 tsp baking powder

¼ tsp baking soda

¼ tsp salt

2 eggs

2 cups/480 ml buttermilk

6 tbsp/85 g unsalted butter, melted and
   slightly cooled

1 cup/115 g pecans, toasted (see cooking tip,
   page 55) and coarsely chopped

1. For the Warm Salted Caramel Sauce: Combine the sugar and water in a heavy, medium saucepan set over low heat, swirling the pan occasionally until the sugar dissolves. Raise the heat and boil, without stirring, until the mixture is syrupy and turns a rich golden brown, 6 to 8 minutes. Remove the pan from the heat and slowly stir in the half-and-half. Be very careful because the mixture will bubble vigorously. Whisk in the butter, and then add the fleur de sel. (The caramel sauce can be prepared 2 days ahead; cool, cover, and refrigerate. Reheat, stirring, over medium heat.) Stir in the bananas. Cover and keep warm.

2. For the Golden Pecan Waffles: Preheat a waffle iron (and, if you plan to hold the waffles until serving time, preheat the oven to 200 degrees F/95 degrees C).

continued . . .

3. In a large bowl, stir together the flour, sugar, baking powder, baking soda, and salt. In another bowl, whisk together the eggs and buttermilk.

4. Make a well in the dry ingredients and pour in the egg mixture, blending gently only until the ingredients are combined. Add the butter in a slow stream, continuing to blend until the butter is incorporated. Fold in the pecans.

5. Pour ½ cup/120 ml of the batter (or more, depending on the size of your waffle iron) onto the waffle iron and, using a metal spatula or table knife, spread the batter to within ½ in/12 mm of the edge. Close the cover and cook approximately 3 minutes, or until crisp and golden brown. (If your waffles aren't crisp, even after a "ready signal" has sounded, continue to cook them, watching carefully, until crisp and golden. If not serving immediately, place the waffles in a single layer on a baking sheet in the preheated oven while you finish with the remaining batter.)

6. Serve waffles topped with several spoonfuls of the warm caramel sauce and bananas.

COOKING TIP:

To toast pecans, spread on a rimmed baking sheet and place in a preheated 350-degree-F/ 180-degree-C/gas-4 oven until fragrant and lightly browned, 6 to 8 minutes. Watch carefully so the nuts do not burn. Remove and cool.

Orange Whole-Wheat Waffles with Yogurt and Fresh Berries

Fresh orange juice and zest add a clear, refreshing accent to these golden-brown waffles, which are prepared with a light version of whole-wheat flour. Dollops of Greek yogurt sweetened with honey and fresh seasonal berries replace the more typical garnishes of maple syrup and butter.

Makes about six 5- to 6-in/12- to 15-cm waffles, to serve 4 to 6

PREP TIME:
25 minutes

START-TO-FINISH TIME:
45 minutes

MAKE AHEAD:
No

Orange Whole-Wheat Waffles

2¼ cups/285 g white whole-wheat flour (see market note)

3 tbsp sugar

2 tsp baking powder

¼ tsp salt

1¼ cups/300 ml whole milk

½ cup/120 ml freshly squeezed orange juice

2 eggs, separated

5 tsp packed grated orange zest

6 tbsp/85 g unsalted butter, melted and slightly cooled

Yogurt Topping

1 cup/240 ml plain Greek-style yogurt (see market note)

4 tsp honey

1 tsp grated orange zest, packed

Fresh raspberries, strawberries, or blueberries, for garnish

 MARKET NOTE:

King Arthur Flour sells an unbleached white whole-wheat flour, which is available in most grocery stores. It's lighter in color than traditional whole wheat and boasts a milder, sweeter flavor. If unavailable, use half whole-wheat and half white flour.

Nonfat, as well as reduced- to whole-fat varieties of Greek yogurt work in this recipe.

1. For the Orange Whole-Wheat Waffles: Preheat a waffle iron (and, if you plan to hold the waffles until serving time, preheat the oven to 200 degrees F/95 degrees C).

2. In a large bowl, stir together the flour, sugar, baking powder, and salt. In another bowl, whisk together the milk, orange juice, egg yolks, and orange zest. In a third bowl, beat the egg whites until firm, but not stiff.

3. Make a well in the dry ingredients and pour in the milk mixture, blending gently only until the ingredients are combined. Add the butter in a slow stream, continuing to blend until the butter is incorporated. Gently fold in the egg whites.

4. For the Yogurt Topping: In a small serving bowl, whisk together the yogurt, honey, and orange zest.

5. Pour ½ cup/120 ml of the batter (or more, depending on the size of your waffle iron) onto the waffle iron and, using a metal spatula or table knife, spread the batter to within ½ in/12 mm of the edge. Close the cover and cook approximately 3 minutes, or until crisp and golden brown. (If your waffles aren't crisp, even after a "ready signal" has sounded, continue to cook them, watching carefully, until crisp and golden. If not serving immediately, place the waffles in a single layer on a baking sheet in the preheated oven while you finish with the remaining batter.)

6. Serve the waffles topped with a generous dollop of the yogurt mixture and garnish with some berries.

Baked Eggnog French Toast with Cranberries and Apples

Crispy baked French toast topped with glistening cranberries and apples makes a stunning main course for a holiday brunch. You can prepare the fruit topping a day ahead and soak the bread slices in eggnog the night before. Either purchased or homemade eggnog (a simple combination of egg yolks, sugar, and cream) will yield delicious results.

Serves 6

PREP TIME:
45 minutes, including making the Glazed Cranberries and Apples, plus 6 hours or longer to refrigerate the toast

START-TO-FINISH TIME:
7 hours or longer

MAKE AHEAD:
Partially

Glazed Cranberries and Apples

2 cups/480 ml apple cider

6 tbsp/90 ml light corn syrup

2 tbsp light brown sugar

8 tbsp/115 g unsalted butter, diced

3 Golden Delicious apples (about 1¼ lb/570 g), peeled, cored, and cut into ½-in/12-mm cubes

2 cups/225 g fresh or frozen cranberries (see market note, page 60)

½ cup/100 g granulated sugar, plus more if needed

Eggnog French Toast

12 thick (¾-in/2-cm) bread slices, cut on a sharp diagonal from a day-old baguette (see market note, page 60)

2½ cups/600 ml purchased eggnog (see cooking tip, page 60)

½ tsp freshly grated nutmeg

Pinch of ground cinnamon

3 tbsp melted unsalted butter

Confectioners' sugar

1. For the Glazed Cranberries and Apples: Whisk together the apple cider, corn syrup, and brown sugar in a large, heavy saucepan set over high heat. Boil until reduced to 1 cup/240 ml, about 15 minutes. Whisk in 4 tbsp/55 g of the butter until melted. Remove from the heat and set aside.

2. Melt the remaining 4 tbsp/55 g butter in a large, heavy frying pan over medium heat until hot. Add the apples and sauté, stirring, for 2 minutes. Add the cranberries and granulated sugar, and stir until the cranberries begin to pop, about 2 minutes. Stir in the reduced cider mixture and cook until the mixture has reduced to a syrup-like consistency, about 6 minutes. Taste and stir in more sugar if desired. (The cranberries and apples can be prepared 1 day ahead; cool, cover, and refrigerate. Reheat, stirring, over medium heat.)

3. For the Eggnog French Toast: Arrange the bread slices in a 9-by-13-in/23-by-33-cm shallow baking dish. Whisk together the eggnog, nutmeg, and cinnamon in a medium bowl. Pour the mixture over the bread. Cover the pan with plastic wrap and refrigerate for 6 hours, or overnight.

continued . . .

4. Arrange a rack at center position and preheat the oven to 450 degrees F/230 degrees C/gas 8. Butter a large, rimmed baking sheet with some of the melted butter. Using a metal spatula, transfer the bread slices to the baking sheet. Brush the bread with the remaining melted butter.

5. Bake for 10 minutes, and then turn and bake until golden brown on the outside and still soft inside, 5 to 6 minutes more. Watch carefully so they do not burn.

6. Arrange two slices on each of six dinner plates and mound the warm fruits on top. Dust generously with confectioners' sugar and serve.

 MARKET NOTE:

If using frozen cranberries, defrost and pat dry.

You can also use a good, crusty sourdough bread; cut ¾-in/2-cm slices from it and, if they are large, cut them in half.

COOKING TIP:

If eggnog is not available at the supermarket, whisk together 4 egg yolks, ½ cup/100 g sugar, and 2 cups/480 ml light cream to blend. Then proceed with the recipe.

Strawberry-Glazed French Toast with Sweetened Sour Cream

Thick slices of good country bread, crisped in the oven before being dipped into a rich vanilla-scented custard mixture, are sautéed slowly in a little butter until rich golden brown. However, what makes this French toast extra-special are the simple toppings. In place of the usual maple syrup, a thin coating of strawberry jam and a dollop of slightly sweetened sour cream add colorful and complementary flavorings.

Serves 4

PREP TIME:
10 minutes

START-TO-FINISH TIME:
45 minutes

MAKE AHEAD:
No

Eight 1-in-/2.5-cm-thick slices bread, cut from a country or peasant loaf (see market note)

2 cups/480 ml half-and-half

4 egg yolks

3 tbsp light brown sugar

1 tbsp vanilla extract, plus ½ tsp

½ tsp cinnamon

3 tbsp unsalted butter

½ cup/120 ml sour cream

1 tbsp granulated sugar

⅓ cup/100 g strawberry jam or preserves (see market note)

 MARKET NOTE:

The best bread for this dish is an unsliced loaf of good-quality peasant or country bread, preferably one without an extra-hard crust. One that is rectangular, rather than round, is more convenient, but either will do. Cut off the ends of the loaf, and reserve for another use. Then slice the bread into 1-in-/2.5-cm-thick slices. If your loaf is large and the slices seem large, cut them in half.

You can try other jams, preserves, or marmalades. Cherry, raspberry, or peach preserves and orange marmalade are other possibilities.

1. Arrange a rack at center position and preheat the oven to 400 degrees F/200 degrees C/gas 6. Place the bread slices on a baking sheet and bake until dry and very lightly browned, about 8 minutes per side. Watch carefully so that the bread does not burn. Remove the bread from the oven and reduce the oven temperature to 200 degrees F/95 degrees C.

2. In a medium bowl, whisk together the half-and-half, egg yolks, brown sugar, 1 tbsp vanilla, and cinnamon. Pour the mixture into a shallow pan (a 9-by-13-in/23-by-33-cm glass baking dish works well). Add the toasted bread slices and soak them for 4 minutes per side. Remove to a large plate or platter.

3. Place a large, heavy frying pan over low to medium heat. Add about 2 tsp of the butter or enough to coat the bottom of the pan lightly. When melted, add enough bread slices to fit comfortably in a single layer. Cook slowly until the slices are golden brown and crisp on both sides, about 4 minutes per side. Remove to a baking sheet and place in the warm oven. Repeat, adding more butter to the pan as needed until all the bread slices have been sautéed.

4. In a small bowl, stir together the sour cream, granulated sugar, and remaining ½ tsp vanilla.

5. When ready to serve, spread each toast with a thin coating of strawberry jam and top with a dollop of sweetened sour cream.

THE BREAD BASKET

Scones, Muffins, Popovers, and Company

Although you might be tempted to run to the bakery or supermarket for a bagful of muffins or scones, with a little extra effort you can pull freshly baked ones from your own oven. Is there anything more welcoming than the aroma of breads wafting through the kitchen? Scrumptious quick breads, like the ones featured in this chapter, can, in most cases, be assembled and baked in the time it would take many of us to drive to the store and back.

These baked goods are termed "quick" because they are leavened with baking powder instead of yeast, which requires long rising times. You simply put the dough or batter together, place it in a pan or on a sheet, and pop it in the oven. For a brunch, it's helpful to have the ingredients for a recipe measured and set out on a kitchen tray. Then at baking time, you'll need only to preheat the oven and do a quick assembly. While quick breads are best piping-hot from the oven, many can be baked ahead and re-warmed, or even served at room temperature.

The mouthwatering offerings on the following pages include a trio of muffins, each with distinctive flavorings. You can choose the extra-moist Tart Cherry and Almond Muffins; savor the ones with lemon, dates, and pecans; or indulge in a batch of gingerbread muffins with a double dose of ginger. There are also tender scones, plus popovers that rise so tall they are described as mile-high, and biscuits as delicate as clouds. A delectable coffee cake, scented with espresso, will feed a crowd—but don't count on any leftovers!

Cranberry-Pecan Scones

The owners of Kinsman Lodge in Franconia, New Hampshire, shared with me the recipe for these popular scones, which they serve at their bed-and-breakfast. What distinguishes these scones is that they are baked with a hearty amount of heavy cream, but no butter or shortening. At the lodge, Sue Thompson varies the dried fruits that stud these tender morning breads, and you can too. I opted for cranberries and also included toasted pecans with a hint of orange to round out the flavors.

Makes 16 scones, to serve 8

PREP TIME:
20 minutes

START-TO-FINISH TIME:
35 minutes

MAKE AHEAD:
Yes

2 cups/225 g cake flour

¼ cup/50 g granulated sugar

1 tbsp baking powder

½ tsp salt

⅔ cup/85 g dried cranberries, coarsely chopped

⅓ cup/35 g pecans, toasted (see cooking tip, page 55) and coarsely chopped

1 tbsp packed grated orange zest

1⅓ cups/315 ml heavy cream, plus 1 tbsp extra if needed, and additional for brushing on tops of scones

1½ to 2 tsp turbinado sugar for garnish (optional; see market note)

 MARKET NOTE:

Turbinado is a raw sugar that has undergone a steam-cleaning process. With its coarse crystals and mild molasses scent, this sugar is good sprinkled on baked goods. It is available at some supermarkets.

1. Arrange a rack at center position and preheat the oven to 400 degrees F/200 degrees C/gas 6. Have ready a large, heavy, ungreased baking sheet.

2. In a large bowl, whisk together the flour, granulated sugar, baking powder, and salt to combine well. Stir in the cranberries, pecans, and orange zest and mix well. Slowly add the 1⅓ cups/315 ml cream into the dry ingredients, while stirring, until the dough comes together. If the dough is dry, add the 1 tbsp cream.

3. On a floured surface, divide the dough in half. Roll each half into a round ¾ in/2 cm thick and about 5½ in/14 cm wide. Cut each round into eight triangles (like you would slice a pizza) and place on the baking sheet. Brush the tops of the scones lightly with cream, and, if desired, sprinkle each with a pinch of turbinado sugar.

4. Bake until light golden brown, 12 to 15 minutes. These scones are best served warm, but they are also good at room temperature. (The scones can be baked 3 to 4 hours ahead; cool, then cover loosely with foil on the baking sheet. Reheat, loosely covered with foil, in a preheated 350-degree-F/180-degree-C/gas-4 oven until just warmed through, 5 to 8 minutes.)

Lemon-Date Muffins with Pecans

Although I baked my first batch of these delectable muffins more than twenty years ago, I find them as tempting today as way back then. It's the fine balance of sweet and tart flavors that makes them distinctive. Chopped pecans and dates offer sweet notes, while a lively hint of lemon is a sharp counterpoint. Although these muffins are delicious when served warm from the oven, they can be baked ahead and reheated with fine results.

Makes 10 to 12 muffins, to serve 6

PREP TIME:
20 minutes

START-TO-FINISH TIME:
45 minutes

MAKE AHEAD:
Yes

6 tbsp/85 g unsalted butter, diced, plus more for the pan

1¾ cups/225 g all-purpose flour, plus more for the pan

2 to 3 thick-skinned lemons

½ cup/100 g firmly packed light brown sugar

¼ cup/60 ml honey

1½ tsp baking powder

½ tsp baking soda

½ tsp salt

½ cup/120 ml sour cream

1 egg

1 cup/170 g chopped dates

⅔ cup/70 g coarsely chopped pecans

¼ cup/60 ml hot water

1. Arrange a rack at center position and preheat the oven to 400 degrees F/200 degrees C/gas 6. Butter and flour the cups of a standard-size muffin pan, use a baking spray, or line them with paper cup liners. Depending on the size of your muffin tins (they can vary from ⅓- to ½-cup/75- to 120-ml capacity), you may get 10 to 12 muffins from the batter.

2. Zest enough lemons to yield 1 tbsp and juice enough to yield 5 tbsp/75 ml.

3. Place the lemon juice, brown sugar, butter, and honey in a medium, heavy saucepan set over medium heat. Stir constantly until the butter has melted and the mixture is well blended and hot, about 2 minutes. Cool slightly.

4. Combine the flour, baking powder, baking soda, and salt in a medium bowl.

5. In a large bowl, whisk together the sour cream, egg, and lemon zest. Whisk in the honey mixture. Stir in the flour mixture until just blended. Add the dates, pecans, and hot water and mix 10 seconds; the mixture will be lumpy. Divide the batter evenly among the prepared muffin cups, filling them three-fourths full.

6. Bake until the muffins are puffed and golden brown, about 20 minutes. Serve warm. (The muffins are best served hot from the oven. However, they can be baked, cooled, covered with foil, and kept at room temperature 4 hours ahead; reheat, wrapped in foil, in a preheated 350-degree-F/180-degree-C/gas-4 oven for 5 to 10 minutes.)

Twice-Ginger Gingerbread Muffins

Gingerbread, that universal favorite, gets a new look and takes far less time to bake when prepared in muffin tins. These irresistible muffins, which rise above the rims of the molds but do not spread out as much as traditional ones, are extra rich and have a deep-brown hue thanks to plenty of dark brown sugar and molasses. There's also a double dose of ginger in these little cakes; ground ginger is added to the batter, and halfway through the baking, chopped crystallized ginger is sprinkled atop each muffin.

Makes about 18 muffins, to serve 9

PREP TIME:
15 minutes

START-TO-FINISH TIME:
50 minutes

MAKE AHEAD:
Yes

12 tbsp/170 g unsalted butter, at room
   temperature, plus more for the pans
2¼ cups/285 g all-purpose flour, plus more
   for the pans
2 tsp ground ginger
1 tsp baking soda
1 tsp cinnamon
½ tsp salt
¼ tsp ground cloves
¼ tsp ground nutmeg
¾ cup/150 g packed dark brown sugar
2 eggs
¾ cup/180 ml unsulphured molasses
1 cup/240 ml boiling water
¾ cup/45 g coarsely chopped crystallized
   ginger

1. Arrange a rack at center position and heat the oven to 350 degrees F/180 degrees C/gas 4. Butter and flour the cups of two standard-size muffin pans, use a baking spray, or line them with paper cup liners. Depending on the size of your muffin tins (they can vary from ⅓- to ½-cup/75- to 120-ml capacity), you may get 18 to 19 muffins from the batter.

2. Sift together the flour, ground ginger, baking soda, cinnamon, salt, cloves, and nutmeg into a medium bowl.

3. Using an electric mixer on medium-high speed, cream the butter and brown sugar until well blended and smooth, about 3 minutes, stopping the mixer and scraping down the sides of the bowl with a spatula if necessary. Add the eggs, one at a time. Then reduce the speed to low and beat in the dry ingredients. Add the molasses and beat for several seconds until blended. Then add the boiling water and beat a few seconds more until blended. Divide the batter evenly among the prepared muffin cups, filling them three-fourths full.

4. Bake until the tops are set but the mixture beneath is jiggly, about 10 minutes. Remove the pans from the oven and sprinkle the crystallized ginger over the top of each muffin. Return to the oven and bake until a tester inserted into the center comes out clean, 9 to 10 minutes more.

5. Remove and cool in the tins for 15 minutes. Serve warm or at room temperature. (The muffins can be prepared 2 days ahead; cool and store in an airtight container at room temperature.)

Tart Cherry and Almond Muffins

Bursting with multiple flavors of cherry, orange, and almond, these muffins are especially moist and turn a beautiful golden brown as they bake. A generous amount of almond paste keeps them from becoming dry, while the dried cherries and orange juice provide tart and sweet notes.

Makes 10 to 12 muffins, to serve 5

PREP TIME:
15 minutes

START-TO-FINISH TIME:
1 hour

MAKE AHEAD:
Yes

6 tbsp/85 g unsalted butter, melted and kept hot, plus more for the pans

1 cup plus 2 tbsp/125 g all-purpose flour, plus more for the pans

6 tbsp/90 ml freshly squeezed orange juice

¾ cup/115 g dried tart cherries

½ cup/100 g sugar

1½ tsp baking powder

¼ tsp salt

One 7-oz/200-g package almond paste, crumbled

3 eggs

1½ tsp grated orange zest

1. Arrange a rack at center position and preheat the oven to 375 degrees F/190 degrees C/gas 5. Butter and flour the cups of a standard-size muffin pan using a baking spray, or line them with paper cup liners. Depending on the size of your muffin tins (they can vary from ⅓- to ½-cup/75- to 120-ml capacity), you may get 10 to 12 muffins from the batter.

2. Bring the orange juice to a simmer in a small saucepan. Remove from the heat and add the cherries; let stand until softened, about 10 minutes.

3. Mix the flour, sugar, baking powder, and salt in a medium bowl. Using an electric mixer, beat the almond paste and melted butter in a large bowl until well blended (the mixture will still have some small pieces of almond paste). Add the eggs, one at a time, beating well after each addition. Mix in the cherry mixture and orange zest. Add the flour mixture and mix until just blended. Divide the batter evenly among the prepared muffin cups, filling them three-fourths full.

4. Bake until a tester inserted into the center of the muffins comes out clean but slightly moist to the touch, about 20 minutes. Serve warm. (The muffins can be prepared 2 days ahead. Cool and wrap the muffins in foil and store at room temperature. Rewarm in the foil in a 350-degree-F/ 180-degree-C/gas-4 oven for 5 minutes.)

Cloud Biscuits

These petite, light-golden biscuits take their name from their soft, airy interiors. They're quite versatile for brunch as they can be served warm in a napkin-lined basket accompanied by butter and good jam, or used for mini-sandwiches. For the latter, fill them with shaved country ham and chutney or pepper jelly, or stuff them with crispy bacon, sharp white cheddar, and sliced apples. During the holidays, thinly sliced turkey, watercress, and cranberry relish make a tempting flavor combination.

*Makes about
20 biscuits, to serve 10*

PREP TIME:
15 minutes

START-TO-FINISH TIME:
30 minutes

MAKE AHEAD:
Yes

3 tbsp unsalted butter, chilled, cut into large pieces, plus more for the baking sheet

2 cups/255 g all-purpose flour

1 tbsp baking powder

½ tsp salt

3 tbsp solid vegetable shortening, cut into large pieces

½ cup plus 2 tbsp/150 ml cold milk, plus more for brushing the biscuits

2 tbsp country-style Dijon mustard

1. Arrange a rack at center position and preheat the oven to 400 degrees F/200 degrees C/gas 6. Lightly butter a large, heavy baking sheet.

2. Combine the flour, baking powder, and salt in a food processor and blend for 5 seconds. Add the butter and shortening and pulse until crumbly, stopping the machine and scraping the sides of the bowl as necessary, about 30 seconds. Transfer to a large bowl.

3. In a small bowl, whisk together the milk and mustard and very gradually pour this over the flour mixture, stirring until just moistened. Turn out the dough onto a floured surface and knead gently just until the dough comes together. Roll out the dough to a thickness of ½ in/12 mm and cut out rounds using a 2-in/5-cm cutter. Gather together the scraps and continue to roll out the dough and cut additional rounds. You should get about 20 biscuits.

4. Place the biscuits 1 in/2.5 cm apart on the prepared baking sheet and brush the tops with additional milk. Bake until light golden, about 14 minutes. Serve warm or at room temperature.

Mile-High Popovers

In my quest for the perfect popover, I had to put in a call to my longtime friend and colleague June McCarthy. The former chef to several Ohio governors, and an especially gifted baker, she did not disappoint. Her popovers, prepared with extra eggs, really do rise sky-high and are richly browned and crisp on the outside, with airy, tender interiors. Don't be tempted to take them out of the oven early, as they need the full baking time to cook all the way through. And while they make a glorious addition to a bread basket, you can also turn them into a main course. Remove their tops and spoon your favorite filling inside, then set the tops back on, slightly askew.

Makes 6 large popovers

PREP TIME:
5 minutes

START-TO-FINISH TIME:
50 minutes

MAKE AHEAD:
No

3 eggs, preferably large

1 cup/240 ml whole milk

4 tbsp/55 g unsalted butter, melted and kept warm

½ tsp salt

1 cup/115 g all-purpose flour

EQUIPMENT NEEDED:

A popover pan with six cups (see cooking tip)

COOKING TIP:

If you don't have popover tins, you can substitute six custard cups that are about 3½ in/9 cm high and 3½ in/9 cm wide at the top. Place them on a rimmed baking sheet and put in the oven for 5 minutes. Continue with the recipe as directed.

1. Arrange a rack at center position and preheat the oven to 425 degrees F/220 degrees C/gas 7. When the oven is ready, place the popover pan in the oven for 5 minutes while you make the batter.

2. In a medium bowl, whisk together the eggs, milk, 3 tbsp of the melted butter, and salt until frothy. Gradually whisk in the flour until the mixture is smooth.

3. Quickly remove the pan from the oven and close the oven door. Immediately drizzle the remaining 1 tbsp butter among the cups. Divide the batter evenly among the cups and put the pan back in the oven, quickly closing the door. Reduce the heat to 375 degrees F/190 degrees C/gas 5 and bake, undisturbed, for 45 minutes.

4. Remove the pan from the oven and serve immediately.

Espresso-Scented Coffee Cake

Lusciously moist and lightly infused with espresso, this dense coffee cake is a definite crowd-pleaser. A mixture of brown sugar, toasted pecans, and butter is used as a filling and also as a topping to add extra flavor and texture. An espresso–cream cheese glaze reinforces the coffee theme. The cake is baked in a 9-in/23-cm springform pan with a small ramekin set in the center—an easy alternative if you do not own a baking pan with a removable tube insert. You can make this tempting confection a day ahead, but you'll need plenty of willpower to resist sneaking a bite!

Serves 8 to 10

PREP TIME:
20 minutes

START-TO-FINISH TIME:
2 hours, including cooling time for the coffee cake

MAKE AHEAD:
Yes

8 tbsp/115 g unsalted butter, chilled and diced, plus more for the pan

2 cups/255 g all-purpose flour

2 cups/400 g light brown sugar

1 tsp cinnamon

¾ cup/85 g pecans, toasted (see cooking tip, page 55) and coarsely chopped

1½ tsp baking powder

¾ tsp baking soda

½ tsp salt

1 cup/240 ml buttermilk

1 egg, at room temperature

1 tbsp instant espresso dissolved in 1 tbsp hot water

1 tsp vanilla extract

Confectioners' sugar

Creamy Espresso Glaze (page 76)

EQUIPMENT NEEDED:

A 9-in/23-cm springform pan and a small ramekin 3 in/7.5 cm in diameter and about 1¾ in/4.5 cm tall (see cooking tip, page 76).

1. Arrange a rack at center position and preheat the oven to 350 degrees F/180 degrees C/gas 4. Butter the bottom and sides of the springform pan and then cut a sheet of parchment paper to fit the bottom of the pan. Place the paper in the pan and then butter the paper. Butter the sides and bottom of the ramekin and place it, right-side up, in the center of the pan.

2. In a large bowl, stir together the flour, brown sugar, and cinnamon. Add the diced butter and rub the mixture between your fingers until it resembles coarse crumbs. Remove ¾ cup/115 g to a small bowl and add the chopped pecans; set aside.

3. Add the baking powder, baking soda, and salt to the large bowl with the flour mixture and stir to combine. In a medium bowl, whisk together the buttermilk, egg, dissolved espresso, and vanilla and then stir them into the dry ingredients just until well blended. The batter should be quite thick.

4. Ladle half of the batter into the prepared pan and spread evenly with a spatula. Sprinkle half of the nut mixture over the batter. Repeat with the remaining batter and nut mixture. Place the pan on a rimmed baking sheet and bake until a tester inserted into the area around the ramekin comes out clean, 40 to 45 minutes.

continued . . .

5. Cool the cake to room temperature, about 45 minutes. Then run a sharp knife around the inside edge of the pan to loosen the cake. Run the knife around the outside of the ramekin to loosen it from the cake. Gently remove the ramekin and the sides of the pan. Dust the cake with confectioners' sugar, drizzle the glaze over the top, and serve.

CREAMY ESPRESSO GLAZE

3 tbsp milk, plus more if needed

1¼ tsp instant espresso powder

3 oz/85 g cream cheese at room temperature, broken into small pieces

⅓ cup/35 g confectioners' sugar

In a medium bowl, whisk together the milk and espresso powder until the espresso has dissolved. Add the cream cheese. With an electric mixer on medium speed, beat the mixture until blended, and then gradually beat in the confectioners' sugar. The glaze should be smooth and thin enough to drizzle over the coffee cake. If too thick, thin with 1 tsp or more of extra milk.

COOKING TIP:

A 3-in/7.5-cm ramekin works best in this recipe. If you use one wider in diameter the space for the batter will be smaller and as the cake cooks some of it is likely to fall into the ramekin. If you have an angel food pan with a removable bottom or a flat-bottomed tube insert for a 9-in/23-cm springform pan, you can use either of those instead.

A squeeze bottle with a small opening makes drizzling the glaze over the coffee cake very easy.

Sausage-Studded Cornbread

Cornbread was a staple at our table when I was growing up in the South. Today, I still use my family's recipe to turn out this quick bread, but often mix in new ingredients. Diced andouille sausage, sautéed and then sprinkled into the batter, is a favorite variation. Bits of Spanish chorizo make an equally tempting addition. Both versions make fine partners to scrambled, poached, or pan-fried eggs.

Serves 8

PREP TIME:
20 minutes

START-TO-FINISH TIME:
40 minutes

MAKE AHEAD:
Yes

2 tbsp vegetable oil, plus 4 tsp

6 oz/330 g andouille sausage or Spanish chorizo (see market note), cut into ¼-in/6-mm dice

2 eggs

¾ cup/180 ml buttermilk

1 cup/140 g yellow cornmeal

¾ tsp baking powder

½ tsp kosher salt

¼ tsp baking soda

 MARKET NOTE:

Use Spanish-style chorizo in casing, not loose Mexican-style chorizo.

1. Arrange a rack at center position and preheat the oven to 450 degrees F/230 degrees C/gas 8.

2. Heat the 2 tbsp vegetable oil until hot in a 9-in/23-cm oven-proof frying pan (preferably a well-seasoned cast-iron one) set over medium-high heat. Add the sausage and sauté until lightly browned, 2 to 3 minutes; drain on paper towels.

3. When the frying pan is cool enough to handle, wipe it out with paper towels. Add the remaining oil to the frying pan and set it over medium-high heat for 2 to 3 minutes just to heat the oil. Remove the frying pan from the heat and set aside.

4. Whisk the eggs and buttermilk in a large mixing bowl. Whisk in the cornmeal, baking powder, salt, and baking soda. Pour the oil from the frying pan into the batter, and mix well. Pour the batter into the frying pan, and sprinkle the cooked sausage evenly over it.

5. Bake the cornbread until it is golden on top and firm to the touch, about 15 minutes. Remove from the oven and run a sharp knife around the edge of the cornbread to loosen it. Invert the pan and turn out the bread onto a rack to cool for about 5 minutes. (The cornbread can be prepared 3 hours ahead. Leave at room temperature. Wrap cornbread in foil and reheat in a preheated 350-degree-F/180-degree-C/gas-4 oven for about 10 minutes.)

FRUITS FOR ALL SEASONS

Fresh, or in Compotes, Parfaits, and Gratins

I can't imagine a brunch without fruit on the menu. Summer berries and melons, autumn apples, or winter's grapefruits and oranges can play a key role at morning meals. Fresh and unadorned or cooked and embellished, they provide bursts of color, interesting textures, and sweetness as well as bracing flavor.

If you are pressed for time, simply slice or dice fresh fruit or use whole berries or grapes. A squeeze of lemon will keep apples and pears from discoloring, while a sprinkle of sugar will sweeten tart berries. Garnish with mint, and you're all set.

If you have just a few extra minutes, though, choose from one of the tempting recipes in this chapter. In warm weather, nothing could be easier or taste better than Summer Berries with Lemon Crème Fraîche or Plum Parfaits with Yogurt and Granola. For those extra-hot days when the temperatures soar, the Duo of Melons with Honey, Lime, and Ginger is exceptionally refreshing. Scrumptious Warm Apple and Date Compotes with Whipped Maple Cream or delectable Wine-Glazed Grapefruit Cups are the answer when it's cold outside.

The recipes that follow have other winning features, especially for the cook. They call for readily available ingredients; they do not require a lot of time; and most can be prepared in advance with just a bit of last-minute attention.

Duo of Melons with Honey, Lime, and Ginger

I first sampled this simple yet exquisite dish at Le Comptoir, one of Paris's most popular Left Bank bistros. As the chef made his rounds to greet guests, I was anxious for him to stop at our table so I could ask if he would share the recipe. He smiled and explained how easy it was to prepare. He had scooped balls from Cavaillon melons (sweeter than but similar to cantaloupes), and then assembled a sauce by puréeing some extra melon with watermelon, lime juice, and honey. For serving, the melon balls were napped with the sauce, and then dusted with freshly grated ginger. At home I used both cantaloupe and watermelon balls for visual contrast, and added candied ginger as a garnish.

Serves 6

PREP TIME:
25 minutes

START-TO-FINISH TIME:
1 hour, 30 minutes;
including 1 hour to
chill the sauce

MAKE AHEAD:
Partially

One medium cantaloupe (about 2½ lb/1.2 kg)

One medium watermelon, preferably seedless
  (about 5 lb/2.3 kg)

¼ cup/60 ml fresh lime juice (3 to 4 limes)

½ cup/120 ml honey

2 tbsp chopped candied ginger

6 mint springs

1. Using a melon baller, scoop out 2 cups/290 g of canta-loupe and 2 cups/360 g of watermelon. Place the balls in a bowl, cover with plastic wrap, and refrigerate until cold, at least 1 hour. (The balls can be prepared up to 6 hours in advance.)

2. Chop 1 cup/145 g of cantaloupe and 1 cup/180 g of water-melon and transfer to a food processor or blender. Add the lime juice and honey and process until the melons are puréed and well blended with the lime juice and honey. Strain the sauce over a 2-cup/480-ml or larger measuring cup with a spout to remove any seeds. Use a spatula to press down on the pulp to release all of the juices. You should get about 2 cups/480 ml sauce. Cover the sauce with plastic wrap and place it in the refrigerator until icy cold, at least 1 hour. (The sauce can be prepared up to 6 hours in advance.)

3. Divide the melon balls evenly among six martini or wide-mouthed wine glasses and pour about ⅓ cup/75 ml of the sauce over each. Sprinkle each serving with 1 tsp candied ginger and garnish each with a mint sprig. Serve cold.

Honey-Roasted Peaches

This simple recipe is perfect to make for a summer brunch when peaches are in their prime. I use yellow ones for their extra shot of color, cutting them into thick wedges before adding seasonings of sugar and lemon. The fruit is spread in a baking dish, topped with honey and butter, and then popped in the oven for less than a half hour. During the final minutes of roasting, chopped almonds and crushed shortbread cookies are sprinkled over the bubbling fruit. Served warm with dollops of crème fraîche, this dish is a tempting version of "peaches and cream."

Serves 4 to 6

PREP TIME:
25 minutes

START-TO-FINISH TIME:
1 hour

MAKE AHEAD:
No

2 tbsp unsalted butter, cut into small pieces, plus more for the baking dish

6 medium peaches, peeled, pitted, and cut into slices ½ in/12 mm thick (about 4 cups/910 g)

3 tbsp sugar

2 tsp grated lemon zest

2 tbsp honey

½ cup/65 g slivered almonds, toasted (see cooking tip) and coarsely chopped

½ cup/40 g crushed shortbread cookies (see market note)

½ cup/120 ml crème fraîche (see cooking tip, page 27)

1. Arrange a rack at center position and preheat the oven to 400 degrees F/200 degrees C/gas 6. Butter a 2-qt/2-L shallow oven-to-table baking dish.

2. In a large bowl, toss together the peaches, sugar, and lemon zest to combine well. Spoon the mixture into the prepared dish. Drizzle the honey over the peaches and dot with the butter. Bake until the peaches are tender and the butter has melted, about 20 minutes.

3. Remove the pan from the oven. Combine the almonds and shortbread and sprinkle over the top. Return the pan to the oven and bake until the topping is light golden brown, about 5 minutes. Remove and cool for 10 minutes.

4. Serve the peaches warm with a dollop of crème fraîche.

 MARKET NOTE:

Be sure to use pure-butter shortbread cookies. They contain enough butter that you don't need to add melted butter to the crumbs for the topping. I like Walkers Shortbread cookies, available in many groceries.

 COOKING TIP:

To toast almonds, spread on a rimmed baking sheet and place in a pre-heated 350-degree-F/180-degree-C/gas-4 oven until lightly browned and fragrant, 6 to 8 minutes. Watch carefully so the nuts do not burn. Remove and cool.

Poached Apricots and Greek Yogurt with Pistachios

I sampled a version of this dish at a restaurant in Boston several years ago, and could not wait to re-create it in my own kitchen. Dried apricots were used in the original, but my version is prepared with fresh ones. Left unpeeled, they are cut in half and simmered quickly in a sugar syrup scented with lemon and ginger. The fruit can be poached a day ahead, so there's no last-minute fuss. At serving time, simply spoon honey-sweetened yogurt into bowls, and top it with the apricots and a sprinkle of chopped pistachios.

Serves 4

PREP TIME:
10 minutes

START-TO-FINISH TIME:
35 minutes, including cooling the poaching liquid

MAKE AHEAD:
Partially

1 lb/455 g apricots, just slightly soft when touched, rinsed and dried, but unpeeled

2 cups/480ml water

¾ cup/150 g sugar

1 tsp grated lemon zest

½ tsp ground ginger

2 tbsp honey

3 cups/720 ml plain Greek-style yogurt (see market note)

4 tbsp/30 g roasted, unsalted pistachios, coarsely chopped

 MARKET NOTE:

Nonfat as well as reduced- to whole-fat varieties of Greek yogurt work in this recipe.

1. Halve the apricots lengthwise, but do not peel them. Remove pits and, if large, cut each half into three wedges.

2. Combine the water, sugar, lemon zest, and ginger in a medium saucepan set over medium-high heat. Stir constantly until the sugar has dissolved, and then bring the mixture to a gentle simmer.

3. Add the apricots and cook until just tender when pierced with a knife, 3 to 4 minutes (depending upon the ripeness of the fruit). Do not overcook or the apricots will become mushy.

4. Remove the pan from the heat and let sit for 2 minutes. Remove the apricots to a bowl using a slotted spoon.

5. Return the poaching liquid to high heat and cook until somewhat syrupy and reduced to about ½ cup/120 ml, 5 to 7 minutes. Cool to room temperature, and then pour over the apricots. (The compote can be prepared 1 day ahead; cool, cover, and refrigerate. Bring to room temperature before using.)

6. Whisk the honey into the yogurt, and divide it among four medium bowls. Top each serving with some apricots and syrup, sprinkle with the pistachios, and serve.

Plum Parfaits with Yogurt and Granola

Made with alternating layers of cooked spiced plums, sweetened yogurt, and granola, all spooned into glasses, these parfaits are a visual feast. The deep crimson-hued fruits make a striking contrast to the pristine whiteness of the yogurt. The plums take about 15 minutes to prep and sauté and will need a few minutes to cool. Then all that is necessary is to whisk the yogurt with some sugar and vanilla and to assemble the parfaits.

Serves 6

PREP TIME:
15 minutes

START-TO-FINISH TIME:
40 minutes, including cooling time for the plums

MAKE AHEAD:
Partially

2 lb/910 g medium-ripe dark red or purple plums, rinsed and dried

1/3 cup/65 g sugar, plus 1½ tbsp, and more if needed

¾ tsp ground ginger

¼ tsp ground cinnamon

2 cups/480 ml plain Greek-style yogurt (see market note)

¼ tsp vanilla extract

¾ cup/85 g granola (see market note)

 MARKET NOTE:

Nonfat as well as reduced- to whole-fat varieties of Greek yogurt work in this recipe.

Use a good-quality purchased granola, preferably one without dried fruits. Maple-flavored ones taste particularly good with the plums and yogurt.

1. Halve the plums lengthwise, and pit. Slice each half, lengthwise, into quarters. Then cut the quarters in half crosswise, if desired.

2. Place a large, heavy frying pan over medium heat until the bottom of the pan is hot. Add the plums and sprinkle with the 1/3 cup/65 g sugar, ginger, and cinnamon. Stir constantly until sugar dissolves and becomes syrupy and the plums are tender when pierced with a knife, about 6 minutes for medium-ripe plums. (If plums are riper, the cooking time will only be about 3 minutes.) Watch carefully so that the fruit does not overcook and become mushy. Remove from the heat and cool the plums to room temperature. If needed, season with more sugar. (The plums can be prepared 1 day ahead; cook, cover, and refrigerate.)

3. In a medium bowl, whisk together the yogurt, 1½ tbsp sugar, and vanilla.

4. Spoon about ¼ cup/60 ml of the plum mixture, including the juices, into each of six medium wine or parfait glasses and top with 2 to 3 tbsp of the sweetened yogurt. Sprinkle with 1 tbsp granola. Repeat this layering one more time in each glass. Serve immediately.

Warm Apple and Date Compotes with Whipped Maple Cream

These delectable compotes are distinguished by their blend of contrasting tastes and textures. Granny Smiths provide tartness to counter the sweetness of the dates, the honey is balanced by lemon juice, and crunchy walnuts are a fine foil to the softly whipped cream. The apples and dates can be cooked and the cream whipped in advance.

Serves 4

PREP TIME:
25 minutes

START-TO-FINISH TIME:
50 minutes

MAKE AHEAD:
Partially

4 medium Granny Smith apples

4 tbsp/55 g unsalted butter

2 tbsp light brown sugar

1 cup/240 ml apple juice

¼ cup/60 ml honey

2 tsp fresh lemon juice

½ tsp cinnamon

¼ tsp ground ginger

8 Medjool dates, pitted and quartered
  lengthwise

Maple Whipped Cream

½ cup/120 ml heavy cream

½ cup/120 ml sour cream

¼ cup/60 ml pure maple syrup

⅓ cup/35 g walnuts, toasted (see cooking tip)
  and coarsely chopped

4 mint sprigs (optional)

🥄 COOKING TIP:

To toast walnuts, spread on a rimmed baking sheet and place in a preheated 350-degree-F/ 180-degree-C/gas-4 oven until fragrant and lightly browned, 6 to 8 minutes. Watch carefully so the nuts do not burn. Remove and cool.

1. Peel and core the apples, and then cut each into eight wedges. Melt the butter in a large, heavy frying pan over medium-low heat. When hot, add the apple wedges and brown sugar. Sauté, turning often, until tender and browned, about 10 minutes. Watch carefully so that the apples do not burn. Remove from the heat and use a slotted spoon to transfer the apples to a platter.

2. Add the apple juice, honey, lemon juice, cinnamon, and ginger to the frying pan and return to medium-low heat. Bring the mixture to a simmer and cook until slightly thickened, 4 to 5 minutes. Add the dates and sautéed apple wedges and cook, stirring, until warmed through, about 2 minutes. Remove from the heat and cover loosely with foil while you prepare the cream. (The fruits can be cooked 1 day ahead; cool, cover, and refrigerate. Reheat, stirring, over medium heat.)

3. For the Maple Whipped Cream: With an electric mixer, whip the cream until firm, and then fold in the sour cream by hand. Gently stir in the maple syrup. (The cream can be prepared 1 day ahead; cover and refrigerate. Whisk gently for a few seconds when ready to use.)

4. Divide the warm apple mixture among four wine or martini glasses. Top each serving with some of the whipped cream and sprinkle with some walnuts. If desired, garnish each serving with a mint sprig before serving.

Summer Berries with Lemon Crème Fraîche

This dish makes a beautiful addition to a spring or summer brunch menu. Although I love to use a mix of seasonal berries, you can opt for a single variety with equally tempting results. The fruit is mounded in wine glasses and topped with spoonfuls of crème fraîche that is scented with lemon and sweetened with a hint of sugar.

Serves 4

PREP TIME:
1 hour, 5 minutes; including chilling time for the crème fraîche

START-TO-FINISH TIME:
1 hour, 10 minutes

MAKE AHEAD:
Partially

Lemon Crème Fraîche

1 cup/240 ml crème fraîche (see cooking tip, page 27)

3½ tbsp sugar

1 tsp grated lemon zest

3 tbsp fresh lemon juice

4 cups/600 g mixed berries such as blueberries, strawberries, raspberries, and blackberries

4 mint sprigs for garnish

1. For the Lemon Crème Fraîche: Place the crème fraîche in a medium, nonreactive bowl. Add the sugar, lemon zest, and lemon juice and whisk well to combine. Cover with plastic wrap and refrigerate until very cold, at least 1 hour. (The crème fraîche can be prepared 2 days ahead; keep covered and refrigerated.)

2. Rinse the berries and gently pat dry. If using strawberries, hull and halve (or quarter if large) lengthwise. Place the berries in a large bowl and gently toss to combine.

3. Divide the berries among four wide-mouthed wine glasses, martini glasses, or dessert bowls. Drizzle each serving with about ¼ cup of the crème fraîche and garnish with a mint sprig. Serve immediately.

Wine-Glazed Grapefruit Cups

Calling for only four simple ingredients, this dish looks and tastes much more sophisticated than you might expect. Ruby Red grapefruit halves are scooped out, mounded with fresh segments, and then drizzled with a garnet-hued syrup made with grapefruit juice, red wine, and sugar. The grapefruit cups can be prepared a day ahead so that at serving time, you will need only to add a colorful garnish of fresh mint.

Serves 6

PREP TIME:
20 minutes

START-TO-FINISH TIME:
30 minutes

MAKE AHEAD:
Yes

5 Ruby Red grapefruit

6 tbsp/90 ml dry red wine

6 tbsp/90 g sugar

6 mint sprigs

1. Halve the grapefruits crosswise and, using a sharp paring knife or a grapefruit knife, remove the segments from each and place them in a medium bowl. By hand, lightly juice the empty grapefruit halves into a small bowl to get 6 tbsp/90 ml of juice; save any extra juice for another use.

2. Using kitchen scissors, trim away and discard the membranes from six of the halves, discarding the other halves. If necessary, cut very thin slices of rind from the bottoms so that the grapefruit halves are not wobbly. Mound the grapefruit segments in the cleaned halves.

3. Combine the grapefruit juice, wine, and sugar in a small, heavy saucepan set over medium-high heat. Stir until the sugar has dissolved. Cook, stirring often, until the mixture has reduced by half and is slightly syrupy, 5 to 8 minutes. Cool to room temperature and then drizzle the syrup over the segments in each grapefruit half. (Grapefruit cups can be prepared 1 day ahead; cover and refrigerate. Bring to room temperature before serving.)

4. Garnish the center of each grapefruit cup with a mint sprig and serve.

BREAKFAST COMPLEMENTS

Potatoes, Bacon, Hash, and Seafood

Although breakfast side dishes are meant to play supporting roles, they are often as important as their main-course counterparts. They round out menus, bringing all the elements together as a whole. Many cooks fall back on predictable brunch extras like bacon, sausages, corned beef hash, and home fries, but there is a host of more creative options. In this chapter, many old standbys get modern updates from assertive seasonings and unexpected ingredient pairings.

Bacon, the quintessential favorite, gets elevated to new heights when it is baked rather than fried, and glazed with an intriguing mix of brown sugar and grainy mustard. All manner of seafood make splendid accompaniments at the brunch table. For an easy, bite-size interpretation of an ever-popular dish, try the Heavenly Little Crab Cakes, which are coated in panko crumbs for extra crispness, scented with citrus, and baked in small muffin tins.

New versions of hash will surprise even your most sophisticated diners, such as one prepared with smoked salmon, fennel, and potatoes and another with sausage, apples, and sage. For new twists on the perennial side of potatoes, there are skillet potatoes with mushrooms and pancetta, and hash browns made from roasted sweet potatoes. Top or pair any with a fried or poached egg for breakfast bliss.

Far from being afterthoughts, these distinctive sides could easily steal the spotlight at your next brunch. Put them at the top of the list when you start to plan your menu.

Roasted Tomatoes on the Vine

For this colorful side dish, I like to use Campari tomatoes, which are about 2 in/5 cm in diameter and usually sold still on the vine. They are tossed in olive oil and dried herbs, and then popped in the oven to roast for less than 15 minutes. Glistening red with slightly puckered skins, they make a delicious garnish for scrambled, fried, or poached eggs.

Serves 4

PREP TIME:
5 minutes

START-TO-FINISH TIME:
20 minutes

MAKE AHEAD:
No

2 tbsp olive oil, plus more for the baking dish
½ tsp dried crushed rosemary (see cooking tip, page 26)
½ tsp dried thyme
Kosher salt
Freshly ground black pepper
1 lb/455 g Campari tomatoes, preferably on the vine (see market note)

 MARKET NOTE:

Campari tomatoes are larger than cherry tomatoes, but smaller than Roma (plum) tomatoes. Deep red in color and often still attached to the vine, they are typically sold packaged in plastic or paper boxes. They are available in most grocery stores year-round.

1. Arrange an oven rack at center position and preheat the oven to 425 degrees F/220 degrees C/gas 7. Lightly grease a medium baking dish with olive oil.

2. In a small bowl, whisk together the 2 tbsp olive oil, rosemary, thyme, ¼ tsp salt, and ¼ tsp pepper. Place the tomatoes in the prepared baking dish and pour the olive oil mixture over them.

3. Roast the tomatoes until they are hot and just starting to shrink, 10 to 12 minutes. Remove from the oven and place on a serving platter. Serve warm.

Roasted Sweet Potato Hash Browns

In this modern take on hash browns, diced sweet potatoes are first roasted to intensify their sweetness, then browned in a hot frying pan, and finally combined with sautéed bacon, red onions, rosemary, and garlic. The three primary ingredients—sweet potatoes, red onions, and bacon—are each easily distinguishable yet complementary to one another.

Serves 4 to 6

PREP TIME:
20 minutes

START-TO-FINISH TIME:
50 minutes

MAKE AHEAD:
Partially

1½ lb/690 g sweet potatoes, peeled and cut into ½-in/12-mm dice

1½ tbsp olive oil

2 tsp dried crushed rosemary (see cooking tip, page 26)

Kosher salt

Coarsely ground pepper

5 thick bacon slices (5½ oz/160 g), cut in 1½-in/4-cm pieces

2 cups/225 g thinly sliced red onion (1 large onion, halved lengthwise and sliced)

2 tsp minced garlic

1 tbsp chopped fresh rosemary, plus a sprig or two for garnish

2 tbsp grated Parmesan cheese (optional)

1. Arrange a rack at center position and preheat the oven to 400 degrees F/200 degrees C/gas 6. Line a large rimmed baking sheet with foil and set aside.

2. Spread the sweet potatoes on the prepared baking sheet. Drizzle with the olive oil and sprinkle the dried rosemary over them. Season with salt and pepper, and then toss to coat evenly.

3. Roast until the potatoes are tender when pierced with a knife, about 20 minutes, stirring after 10 minutes. Remove from the oven when done. (The potatoes can be prepared 2 hours ahead; leave loosely covered with foil at room temperature.)

4. While the potatoes are in the oven, cook the bacon in a large, heavy frying pan over medium-low heat until crisp. Drain on paper towels. Remove all but 1 tbsp of the drippings from the frying pan; reserve the remaining drippings. Place the frying pan on medium to medium-low heat and add the onion. Cook, stirring often, until lightly browned, about 6 minutes. Add the garlic and cook just until fragrant, about 1 minute more.

5. Remove the onion and garlic from the pan. Add 1 to 2 tbsp of the reserved bacon drippings back to the hot frying pan. Add the sweet potatoes and quickly sauté until crisp and nicely browned, 2 to 3 minutes. Return the onion, garlic, and bacon pieces to the frying pan and stir 1 minute more. Season with fresh rosemary, ½ tsp salt, and 1 tsp pepper. For a slightly richer taste, toss the mixture with the Parmesan. Serve warm, garnished with the rosemary sprigs.

Skillet-Roasted Potatoes with Mushrooms and Pancetta

A single pan is all you need to prepare this glorious dish. Baby potatoes, brown mushrooms, and pancetta are sautéed, then roasted, and finally served in one large, heavy frying pan. The golden potatoes and tender mushrooms, seasoned with thyme and garlic, make a mouthwatering garnish to fried, poached, or scrambled eggs.

Serves 4

PREP TIME:
15 minutes

START-TO-FINISH TIME:
45 minutes

MAKE AHEAD:
No

4 oz/115 g pancetta, cut into ¼-in/
    6-mm cubes (see market note)

3 tbsp olive oil, plus more if necessary

1 lb/455 g baby Yukon gold potatoes,
    unpeeled, scrubbed, and quartered

Kosher salt

Freshly ground black pepper

10 oz/280 g cremini or brown mushrooms,
    quartered

6 garlic cloves, peeled and halved crosswise

2 tsp dried thyme

Several fresh thyme sprigs for garnish
    (optional)

 MARKET NOTE:

If buying pancetta from a deli, ask for it to be cut thickly into ¼-in/6-mm slices. Prepackaged pancetta is often thinly sliced.

1. Arrange a rack at center position and preheat oven to 400 degrees F/200 degrees C/gas 6.

2. In a large, heavy, ovenproof frying pan (preferably cast iron) set over medium heat, sauté the pancetta until golden and crisp, 5 to 7 minutes. Remove with a slotted spoon to drain on paper towels.

3. Remove all but 2 tbsp of the drippings from the pan. (If you don't have 2 tbsp, add olive oil to make this amount.) When hot, add the potatoes and sauté, stirring, until they start to take on a little color, 5 to 7 minutes. Season with salt and pepper and place the frying pan in the oven. Roast for 15 minutes.

4. Remove the frying pan from the oven and add the mushrooms, garlic, and the 3 tbsp olive oil. Add the dried thyme and season with more salt and pepper. Toss to coat well.

5. Return the pan to the oven and roast until the potatoes are golden brown and tender and the mushrooms are softened, 15 minutes more. Remove the frying pan from the oven and stir in the reserved pancetta. If desired, garnish the center of the pan with fresh thyme sprigs. Serve warm.

Southern Cheese Grits

Grits, that staple of Southern cooking, were a frequent side dish at morning meals when I was growing up in Memphis. On weekdays, my mother cooked grits in simmering water until they thickened into a creamy porridge, and served them with pats of butter. For special occasions she embellished them with cheeses and seasonings, and spooned them into a casserole to bake, as in this recipe. Cheddar and Parmesan cheeses enrich these grits and add to their smoothness, while cayenne and black pepper provide a bit of heat. Easy to prepare ahead, these grits are a stellar accompaniment to scrambled or poached eggs.

Serves 4 to 6

PREP TIME:
10 minutes

START-TO-FINISH TIME:
55 minutes

MAKE AHEAD:
Partially

Unsalted butter, for the baking dish

4 cups/960 ml water

1 cup/170 g old-fashioned (not instant or quick) grits (see cooking tip)

Salt

¾ cup/60 g grated sharp white cheddar cheese

½ cup/60 g grated Parmesan cheese

½ tsp freshly ground black pepper

⅛ tsp cayenne pepper

COOKING TIP:

If using stone-ground grits, be sure to follow the package directions as they may call for a different amount of water and a longer cooking time.

---

1. Butter a shallow, 2-qt/2-L oven-to-table baking dish.

2. Bring the water to a boil in a large, heavy saucepan (with a lid) set over medium-high heat. Pour the grits in slowly. Add ¾ tsp salt and whisk well.

3. When the mixture comes to a simmer, reduce the heat to low and cover the pan. Cook the grits at a gentle simmer, stirring every 3 to 4 minutes, so they do not stick to the bottom of the pan. Cook until the grits have thickened, about 15 minutes or according to package directions.

4. Remove the grits from the heat and stir in ½ cup/40 g of the cheddar and all of the Parmesan. Add the black pepper and cayenne and season with more salt, if needed. Spread the grits in an even layer in the prepared pan and sprinkle the remaining ¼ cup/20 g cheddar over the top. (The grits can be prepared 1 day ahead; cool, cover, and refrigerate. Bring to room temperature before baking.)

5. Arrange a rack at center position and preheat the oven to 350 degrees F/180 degrees C/gas 4. Bake the grits until they are hot and the cheese has melted on top, 25 minutes. If you would like to brown the cheese, arrange an oven rack 4 to 5 in/10 to 12 cm from the broiler and broil until the cheese starts to brown lightly, 2 to 3 minutes. Serve immediately.

Bacon with a Brown Sugar–Mustard Glaze

The combination of salty, sweet, and tart provided respectively by the bacon, brown sugar, and mustard is what makes this dish so tempting. Baking the strips is another bonus since it requires less attention than pan-frying and eliminates splattering. A simple paste of sugar and mustard is brushed on the strips once they are browned. This recipe can easily be doubled (see cooking tip).

Serves 4

PREP TIME:
5 minutes

START-TO-FINISH TIME:
25 minutes

MAKE AHEAD:
No

2 tbsp light brown sugar

1 tbsp country-style Dijon mustard

8 thick slices bacon (10 oz/290 g)

COOKING TIP:

If you want to double this recipe, use two baking sheets and two racks, placing one sheet in the top third of the oven and the other in the center. Watch carefully, and reverse the racks after the first 10 minutes of cooking, when you turn the bacon with tongs.

You can use this glaze on other breakfast meats. Try it on thick slices of pan-fried ham or breakfast sausages. Brush the glaze on the meat during the last 30 seconds of cooking.

1. Arrange a rack at center position and preheat the oven to 400 degrees F/200 degrees C/gas 6. Have ready a rimmed baking sheet with a footed rack.

2. In a small bowl, whisk together the brown sugar and mustard until the sugar has blended into the mustard to form a thin paste.

3. Arrange the bacon in a single layer on the rack set in the baking sheet and place it in the oven. Bake for 10 minutes and then turn the slices with tongs. Bake until the slices begin to brown, 5 minutes more.

4. Remove the pan from the oven and brush the glaze on the slices. Return to the oven and bake until crisp, 3 to 5 minutes more. Serve immediately.

Smoked Sausage and Apple Hash

Bits of kielbasa, diced apples, and chopped onions, lightly caramelized and seasoned with fresh sage and a hint of grainy Dijon mustard, combine to make a winning trio for this delectable hash. This dish can be prepared several hours ahead, and needs only a quick reheating at serving time.

Serves 6

PREP TIME:
15 minutes

START-TO-FINISH TIME:
35 minutes

MAKE AHEAD:
Yes

4 tbsp/55 g unsalted butter

1½ cups/190 g chopped onion

2 Gala apples, unpeeled, cored, cut into
½-in/12-mm pieces (about 3½ cups)

1 lb/455 g kielbasa or other cooked smoked
sausage, cut into ½-in/12-mm dice (about
2½ cups)

Packed 2 tbsp finely julienned sage leaves

2 tsp country-style Dijon mustard

Kosher salt

Freshly ground black pepper

1. In a large, heavy frying pan set over low heat, melt the butter. Raise the heat to medium and add the onion. Cook, stirring often, until the onion is just softened but not browned, about 4 minutes. Add the apples and cook until barely starting to soften, another 4 minutes.

2. Add the smoked sausage and cook and stir until the sausage, onion, and apples are all browned lightly and starting to caramelize, about 10 minutes. (The hash can be prepared 4 hours ahead; leave at room temperature. Reheat, uncovered, over medium heat, stirring constantly.) Stir in the sage and mustard and remove from the heat. Taste and, if needed, season with salt and pepper. Serve warm.

Smoked Salmon, Fennel, and Potato Hash

There are many delicious alternatives to traditional corned beef hash. This one, for example, pairs flaked hot-smoked salmon with sautéed fennel, onions, and potatoes. Crushed fennel seeds and chopped lacy fennel fronds add a mild anise flavor. Topped with a poached egg, this dish becomes a main course.

Serves 6

PREP TIME:
15 minutes

START-TO-FINISH TIME:
45 minutes

MAKE AHEAD:
No

1 lb/455 g Russet or Yukon gold potatoes, peeled and cut into ½-in/12-mm cubes

Kosher salt

2 medium fennel bulbs with their lacy stalks

¼ cup/60 ml olive oil

1 cup/125 g chopped onion

½ lb/225 g hot-smoked salmon fillet, skin discarded and salmon flaked (see market note, page 101)

1 tsp fennel seeds, crushed (see cooking tip, page 101)

Freshly ground black pepper

1. Bring a large saucepan filled two-thirds full with water to a boil. Add the potatoes and 2 tsp salt. Cook until the potatoes are tender when pierced with a knife but still hold their shape, about 5 minutes. Drain the potatoes in a colander and set aside.

2. Cut off the stalks from the fennel bulbs. Remove the thin lacy fronds and chop enough of them to make 2 tbsp; set aside. Reserve a few lacy sprigs in a glass of water for the garnish. Halve the bulbs lengthwise, and with a sharp knife, cut out and discard the tough triangular cores. Then chop enough fennel to yield 2 cups/260 g. Save any extra for another use.

3. Add half of the olive oil to a large, heavy frying pan set over medium heat. Add the chopped fennel and onion and cook, stirring often, until softened and lightly browned around the edges, 4 to 5 minutes. Remove to a plate.

continued . . .

4. Heat the remaining oil in the same frying pan and, when hot, add the potatoes. Cook, stirring occasionally, until the potatoes are golden brown, 8 to 10 minutes.

5. Return the fennel and onion to the frying pan and stir 1 minute to reheat. Add the flaked salmon and the crushed fennel seeds and cook 1 minute more. Season the hash with more salt and with several generous grinds of pepper. Sprinkle with the reserved chopped fennel fronds.

6. Mound the hash in a serving dish and garnish the center with some fennel sprigs. Serve warm.

 MARKET NOTE:

There are two basic ways of smoking salmon—cool smoked and hot smoked. The former, usually sold thinly sliced, has a delicate smoked flavor and is readily available in many groceries. The hot-smoked variety is typically cut thicker, is firmer, and has an intense smoky flavor. Hot-smoked salmon is sold in some supermarkets such as Whole Foods, and comes plain and sometimes scented with light maple, pepper, or other seasonings. The plain or light maple-flavored varieties work well in this recipe.

 COOKING TIP:

To crush fennel seeds, place them in a self-sealing bag and pound with a meat pounder or rolling pin, or use a mortar and pestle. Or, use a small spice grinder and grind the seeds coarsely.

Smoked Salmon with Herbed Crème Fraîche

This side dish requires no cooking at all. You simply arrange slices of smoked salmon on a platter, and scatter some sliced red onion over the fish. Accompaniments include a bowl of crème fraîche scented with lemon, chives, and tarragon and a basket of good dark bread.

Serves 6 to 8

PREP TIME:
10 minutes, plus
1 hour chilling time
for the crème fraîche

START-TO-FINISH TIME:
1 hour, 15 minutes

MAKE AHEAD:
Partially

¾ cup/180 ml crème fraîche (see cooking tip, page 27)

¾ tsp fresh lemon juice

½ tsp finely grated lemon zest

10 to 12 oz/280 to 336 g thinly sliced smoked salmon

¼ cup/30 g thinly sliced red onion (1 small onion, halved lengthwise and sliced)

Freshly ground black pepper

1½ tsp finely chopped fresh chives

1½ tsp finely chopped fresh tarragon

Crusty whole-wheat, multigrain, or peasant loaf made with whole-wheat flour, sliced, each slice quartered

1. In a small serving bowl, whisk together the crème fraîche, lemon juice, and lemon zest. Cover and chill for at least 1 hour. (The herbed crème fraîche can be made 1 day ahead; cover and refrigerate.)

2. Arrange overlapping salmon slices on a platter. Sprinkle the onion slices over the fish and season generously with several grinds of black pepper. (The salmon can be prepared 4 hours ahead; cover and refrigerate.)

3. Stir 1 tsp of the chives and 1 tsp of the tarragon into the crème fraîche mixture; sprinkle the remaining herbs over the top of the crème fraîche. Arrange the bread in a napkin-lined basket. Serve the salmon on bread slices garnished with a generous dollop of crème fraîche.

Heavenly Little Crab Cakes

Baked rather than fried, these crab cakes are small enough to eat in a single bite. They have a golden, crisp coating and are lusciously smooth inside. The crunchy exteriors come from a mixture of panko crumbs and grated Parmesan that is pressed onto the bottoms of mini-muffin tins. A melange of fresh crab, cream cheese, and citrus zests is spooned on top and covered with more panko mix. These miniature crab cakes, which need about a half hour in the oven, are equally good as sides or as openers for a brunch menu.

Makes 24 crab cakes, to serve 8

PREP TIME:
20 minutes

START-TO-FINISH TIME:
1 hour, 20 minutes

MAKE AHEAD:
Yes

8 oz/226 g cream cheese, at room temperature

¾ cup/90 g finely grated Parmesan cheese

1 egg

¼ cup/60 ml sour cream

1 tsp grated orange zest

½ tsp grated lemon zest

4 tbsp chopped chives

Generous ¼ tsp kosher salt

Generous pinch of cayenne pepper

6 oz/170 g fresh crabmeat, preferably unpasteurized, drained well (see market note, page 105)

4 tbsp/55 g unsalted butter, melted, plus more for the muffin tins

1 cup/115 g panko crumbs

¼ cup/60 ml purchased mayonnaise

1 tsp Dijon mustard

EQUIPMENT NEEDED:
Two nonstick 12-cup mini-muffin tins

1. With an electric mixer on medium speed, beat the cream cheese until smooth, about 2 minutes. Add ¼ cup/30 g of the Parmesan and the egg. Continue to beat until blended, about 1 minute. Add the sour cream, orange and lemon zests, 1 tbsp of the chives, the salt, and cayenne. Beat until combined well, about 30 seconds, and then fold in the crabmeat. (The filling can be made 1 day ahead; cover and refrigerate. Bring to room temperature before using.)

2. Arrange a rack at center position and preheat the oven to 350 degrees F/180 degrees C/gas 4. Butter the muffin tins generously.

3. Place the panko crumbs, remaining ½ cup/60 g Parmesan, and 2 tbsp of the chives in a small bowl. Add the 4 tbsp/55 g melted butter and toss with a fork until evenly moistened. Press 1 tbsp of the panko mixture onto the bottom of each muffin cup, and then spoon 1 tbsp of the crab mixture into each. Sprinkle a generous 1 tsp of the panko mixture over each. (You may have some panko mixture left over.)

continued . . .

4. Bake the crab cakes until golden and set, 25 to 30 minutes. Remove and cool in pans for 5 minutes. Run a small sharp knife around each crab cake and gently lift it out. (The crab cakes can be prepared 2 hours ahead; arrange on a baking sheet and let stand uncovered at room temperature. Rewarm in a preheated 350-degree-F/180-degree-C/gas-4 oven for 6 to 8 minutes.)

5. Arrange the crab cakes (bottom-sides up) on a serving platter. Whisk the mayonnaise and mustard together and place a small dollop on top of each crab cake. Sprinkle the crab cakes with the remaining chives. Serve warm.

 MARKET NOTE:

Fresh crabmeat works best in this recipe. If you use pasteurized crab, drain it well and press to remove any excess moisture.

DRINKS,
CLASSIC AND NEW

Perfect for Toasting and Sipping

Whether you are popping Champagne corks or squeezing oranges for a pitcher of fresh juice, give some thought to refreshments when planning a brunch. Spirited or not, what you pour at these morning gatherings should be special. Along with good coffee and tea, there are scores of possibilities for drinks that are mixed, brewed, mulled, and juiced, all with delicious results.

On the following pages, you'll find two additions to Champagne that make it even more festive. For one version, a few spoonfuls of raspberry purée are stirred into a flute of bubbly, instantly turning it a deep crimson hue and supplying an extra fruity accent. In another, elderflower liqueur, a popular French product, provides an amazing floral note. You'll also find the directions for those perennial brunch libations, Bloody Marys and mimosas.

Fresh Citrus Spritzers, prepared with both orange and lemon juices plus sugar syrup, are as cooling as their name implies, while warm mulled cider with spices will stave off autumn's chill. On those extra-cold days, you can finish a morning meal with cups of steaming hot Irish coffee.

Chilled or warm, these beverages will definitely enliven any brunch. Some make fine beginnings, and others perfect endings. Cheers!

Fresh Citrus Spritzers

One of my friends describes this drink as a glassful of sunshine. She is right. There's a bright, shining quality to both the look and taste of these spritzers. The tangy combination of freshly squeezed orange and lemon juices with citrus-infused sugar syrup and sparkling water results in a morning beverage that is cool, crisp, and refreshing.

Makes 1 qt/960 ml, to serve 4 to 6

PREP TIME:
10 minutes

START-TO-FINISH TIME:
40 minutes

MAKE AHEAD:
Partially

4 to 5 navel oranges, plus thin orange slices for garnish

2 to 3 lemons

⅔ cup/165 ml water

¼ cup/50 g sugar

2 cups/480 ml Perrier or other sparkling water, chilled

COOKING TIP:

You can add dry white wine to these spritzers for a more spirited drink. Use 1 part spritzer to 1 part white wine. Pinot Grigio is a particularly good choice.

1. With a swivel peeler, remove the peel (avoiding the white pith beneath the skin) from 2 of the oranges and 2 of the lemons. Place the peels, water, and sugar in a medium saucepan set over medium heat. Bring the mixture to a boil, stirring until the sugar dissolves. Boil gently until the syrup is infused with the orange and lemon flavors, about 3 minutes. Remove the pan from the heat and let the syrup steep for 5 minutes. Transfer the syrup and the peels to a bowl and refrigerate until just cooled, about 10 minutes.

2. Halve the fruits and juice them, to yield 1 cup/240 ml fresh orange juice and ½ cup/120 ml fresh lemon juice. (Both the syrup and the juices can be prepared 1 day ahead; cover and refrigerate.)

3. When ready to serve, strain the sugar syrup over a small bowl, pressing on the peels to extract as much liquid as possible. Combine the strained syrup, juices, and Perrier in a pitcher, and stir to mix.

4. Pour into wine glasses filled with ice. Garnish each glass with an orange slice and serve.

Champagne Two Ways

The French love to start meals, including brunch, with Champagne. They sip their bubbly plain and also add embellishments. The two French variations that follow—one enhanced by fresh raspberry purée, the other by a delicious elderflower liqueur—turn simple glasses of Champagne into something extra special.

PREP TIME:
5 minutes

START-TO-FINISH TIME:
10 minutes

MAKE AHEAD:
No

CHAMPAGNE WITH ST. GERMAIN

Serves 1

One part elderflower liqueur (see market note)

Three parts Champagne

Fresh strawberry or raspberry (optional)

Pour the elderflower liqueur into a champagne flute. Tilt the glass and add the Champagne. If desired, float a small strawberry as a garnish before serving.

 MARKET NOTE:

St. Germain, a French brand of elderflower liqueur, is available in shops that sell wines and spirits.

CHAMPAGNE WITH RASPBERRIES

Serves 6

2 cups/300 g fresh raspberries, plus more berries for garnish

2 tbsp sugar

One 750-ml bottle Champagne

Place the raspberries and sugar in a food processor and pulse until the mixture is puréed. Strain over a small bowl to remove the seeds. Divide the strained purée evenly among six champagne flutes. Fill the glasses two-thirds full with Champagne. Drop some raspberries in each flute as a garnish and serve.

Classic Mimosas

Fresh chilled orange juice and icy cold Champagne are a match made in heaven. The name for this wildly popular brunch drink, created in the early part of the twentieth century, is a reference to the yellow flowers of the mimosa plant. The Paris Ritz Hotel served mimosas in the 1920s and, around the same time, London's Buck's Club offered a similar cocktail of orange juice and sparkling wine called Buck's Fizz.

Serves 1

PREP TIME:
5 minutes

START-TO-FINISH TIME:
5 minutes

MAKE AHEAD:
No

For a stronger taste of orange:
One part chilled fresh orange juice
One part chilled Champagne

or

For a stronger taste of Champagne and more fizz:
One part chilled fresh orange juice
Three parts chilled Champagne

Pour the orange juice into a champagne flute. Tilt the glass and fill with champagne. Serve immediately.

Bellinis

The Bellini, a 1948 creation of Giuseppe Cipriani, owner of Venice's celebrated Harry's Bar, was named for Giovanni Bellini, a fifteenth-century Venetian painter. The original version, a pairing of puréed white peaches and prosecco, was served only when this sweet fruit was in season. Later, after the Cipriani family established a New York outpost, they discovered a frozen white peach purée that enabled them to offer the popular drink year-round. For home cooks, the purée is a breeze to put together in a blender or processor. Sweetened with a little sugar and seasoned with lemon juice, it can be assembled with white or yellow peaches. Cool, refreshing, and visually tempting, Bellinis make welcoming openers for any brunch.

Serves 6

PREP TIME:
10 minutes

START-TO-FINISH TIME:
15 minutes

MAKE AHEAD:
Partially

2 ripe peaches (9½ oz/270 g), yellow or white (see market note), plus 6 peach wedges, peeled, for garnish (optional)

2 tbsp fresh lemon juice

1 tsp sugar

One 750-ml bottle prosecco

MARKET NOTE:

If you can't find fresh, ripe peaches, you can substitute frozen ones. Make certain they are unsweetened, and pat dry with paper towels once they have been defrosted. Count on 1½ cups/345 g sliced peaches to replace 2 peaches.

1. Peel the peaches, pit them, and cut into wedges. Place in a blender or food processor along with the lemon juice and sugar. Process until the mixture is a smooth purée. (The purée can be prepared 3 hours ahead; cover and refrigerate until ready to use.)

2. Divide the peach purée evenly among six champagne flutes. Fill each flute about two-thirds full with prosecco. Stir to combine. If desired, garnish the rim of each glass with a peach wedge. Serve immediately.

Bloody Marys

The Bloody Mary, that always fashionable brunch opener, has an interesting history. The most common legend is that bartender Fernand Petiot served it in the 1920s at Harry's New York Bar in Paris, and then brought the drink to New York City in the 1930s when he took a job at the St. Regis's King Cole Bar. The origin of the name is also ambiguous, but it is often attributed to Queen Mary I of England. The following version has plenty of spicy notes, a cooling hint of citrus from lime, and a touch of heat from Tabasco. Serve it without liquor as a Virgin Mary, or as an "Experienced" Bloody Mary with a shot of vodka.

Serves 6

PREP TIME:
10 minutes

START-TO-FINISH TIME:
15 minutes

MAKE AHEAD:
Yes

Virgin Marys

1 recipe Mary Mix (recipe follows)

6 lime wedges

Six 1-in/2.5-cm pieces of celery

Experienced Bloody Marys

1 recipe Mary Mix (recipe follows)

6 lime wedges

Six 1-in/2.5-cm pieces of celery

9 oz/270 ml vodka

For Virgin Marys: Add the mix to six 10- to 12-oz/300- to 360-ml glasses filled with ice. Spear a lime wedge and a piece of celery on each of six skewers for the garnish. Serve immediately.

For Experienced Bloody Marys: Prepare as directed, but stir 1½ oz/45 ml of vodka into each glass before serving.

Mary Mix

1½ cups/360 ml tomato juice

1½ cups/360 ml V8 juice

1½ tbsp prepared horseradish

1½ tbsp Worcestershire sauce

1 tbsp freshly squeezed lime juice

¾ tsp freshly ground black pepper

¾ tsp Tabasco sauce

⅜ tsp celery salt

Add all of the ingredients to a large pitcher. Stir well to mix. The mix can be made 1 day ahead and refrigerated.

Warm Fall Cider with Spices

When fresh cider appears on the market shelves, buy some to make this delectable warm brew, perfect for serving at a fall brunch. It takes only a few minutes to simmer the cider with melted butter, brown sugar, and spices. Dark rum and sliced apples and oranges round out the flavorings.

Makes 10 servings

PREP TIME:
15 minutes

START-TO-FINISH TIME:
30 minutes

MAKE AHEAD:
Yes

2 qt/2 L fresh apple cider

4 tbsp/55 g unsalted butter

½ cup/100 g firmly packed dark brown sugar

10 thin orange slices, cut in half

½ apple, cored but not peeled, cut into thin slices

3 cinnamon sticks, 2 to 3 in/5 to 7.5 cm long, broken in half, plus 10 extra for garnish

4 whole cloves

½ tsp ground ginger

¼ tsp grated nutmeg

½ cup/120 ml dark rum (see market note)

🟦 MARKET NOTE:

Dark rather than light rum, such as Myers's, works best in this recipe. You can omit the rum for a nonalcoholic preparation, and it will still taste good.

1. Place the cider in a large saucepan set over medium heat and heat until it is warmed through.

2. While the cider is heating, melt the butter in a large, heavy saucepan set over medium heat.

3. When the butter is melted, add the brown sugar and stir for about 1 minute. (The sugar will not be completely dissolved.) Add the warm cider and stir until all the sugar has dissolved into the liquid.

4. Add half of the orange slices, the apple slices, the halved cinnamon sticks, cloves, ginger, nutmeg, and rum. Stir and cook at a simmer, until the flavors have melded well, 8 to 10 minutes. (The cider can be prepared 2 days ahead; cool, cover and refrigerate. Reheat over medium heat, stirring often.)

5. Ladle the warm cider into mugs or cups. Garnish each mug with an orange slice and a cinnamon stick and serve.

Irish Coffee

Irish Coffee, as the legend goes, found its way from the airport in Shannon, Ireland, to the Buena Vista bar in San Francisco in the 1950s. The drink was given to weary passengers in the airport before their travels, and a San Franciscan brought the recipe home to share. Irish whiskey, sugar, and some good strong coffee make up the celestial trinity. Softly whipped cream makes an irresistible topping.

Serves 4

PREP TIME:
5 minutes

START-TO-FINISH TIME:
10 minutes

MAKE AHEAD:
No

¼ cup/60 ml good quality Irish whiskey
  (Jameson's works well)

8 tsp sugar

1⅓ cups/315 ml brewed hot coffee, preferably
  strong, dark French roast

½ cup/120 ml heavy cream, whipped softly

1. Place 1 tbsp whiskey and 2 tsp sugar in each of four 8-oz/240-ml glasses or cups. Stir with a spoon until the sugar dissolves. Pour enough hot coffee into each glass or cup to fill it about three-fourths full.

2. Hold a tablespoon (with the back of the spoon facing you) over the coffee in one cup and ladle 2 to 3 tbsp of the whipped cream over the spoon so that it gently falls into the coffee. Adding the cream this way will help it float on top of coffee instead of sinking immediately to the bottom. Repeat with the three other servings. Serve immediately.

THE BRUNCH PLANNER

HOLIDAY BRUNCHES

CHRISTMAS MORNING BRUNCH—BEFORE OR AFTER THE PRESENTS

Classic Mimosas (page 112) or freshly squeezed orange juice

Gratin of Eggs, Leeks, Bacon, and St. André Cheese (page 35)

Wine-Glazed Grapefruit Cups (page 89)

NEW YEAR'S DAY BRUNCH

Champagne with St. Germain (page 110)

10-Minute Blini (page 48) with smoked salmon, red onions, and sour cream

Herbed Scrambled Eggs Nestled in Broiled Portobellos (page 23)

Roasted Tomatoes on the Vine (page 92)

Bowl of clementines or blood oranges

BRUNCH FOR EASTER MORNING

Fresh Citrus Spritzers (page 109)

Eggs Baked with Crème Fraîche, Crab, and Tarragon (page 27)

Salad of watercress, cucumber, and radishes in vinaigrette

Tart Cherry and Almond Muffins (page 70)

THANKSGIVING BRUNCH FOR WEEKEND COMPANY

Baked Eggnog French Toast with Cranberries and Apples (page 59)

Bacon with a Brown Sugar–Mustard Glaze (page 97)

Platter of orange and red grapefruit slices with fresh mint

A BRUNCH FOR EVERY SEASON

FOR CRISP AUTUMN DAYS

Warm Fall Cider with Spices (page 115)

Caramelized Shallot and Ham Tartlets (page 41)

Frisée salad in vinaigrette

Warm Apple and Date Compotes with Whipped Maple Cream (page 86)

FOR COLD WINTER DAYS

Smoked Sausage and Apple Hash (page 98) topped with poached eggs (see page 13)

Mile-High Popovers (page 73)

Plum Parfaits with Yogurt and Granola (page 84)

FOR WARMING SPRING DAYS

Heavenly Little Crab Cakes (page 103)

Parmesan Flans with Parmesan Crisps (page 39)

Roasted or blanched asparagus dusted with fleur de sel

Lemon-Date Muffins with Pecans (page 66)

FOR LAZY SUMMER DAYS

Bellinis (page 113)

Grape Tomato and Blue Cheese Tart (page 42)

Platter of thinly sliced prosciutto or serrano ham with fresh figs

Duo of Melons with Honey, Lime, and Ginger (page 80)

BRUNCHES WITH A PURPOSE

KIDS IN THE KITCHEN

Freshly squeezed orange or grapefruit juice

Spiced Pancakes with Warm Maple-Butter Syrup (page 49)

Bacon with a Brown Sugar–Mustard Glaze (page 97)

Summer Berries with Lemon Crème Fraîche (page 87)

BRUNCH FOR A CROWD

Champagne Two Ways (page 110)

Gratin of Eggs, Leeks, Bacon, and St. André Cheese (page 35)

Cloud Biscuits (page 71) filled with ham, orange marmalade, and fresh mint

Baby spinach, belgian endive, and toasted walnut salad in vinaigrette

Espresso-Scented Coffee Cake (page 74)

BRUNCH IN A HURRY

Freshly squeezed grapefruit juice

Smoked Salmon with Herbed Crème Fraîche (page 102)

Poached Eggs, Asparagus, and Chorizo (page 19)

Platter of sliced cantaloupe and honeydew drizzled with lime juice

BRUNCH WITH A HEALTHY ANGLE

Fresh Citrus Spritzers (page 109)

Orange Whole-Wheat Waffles with Yogurt and Fresh Berries (page 57)

Pan-grilled chicken or turkey sausage

Duo of Melons with Honey, Lime, and Ginger (page 80) with fresh figs

INDEX